1001
QUESTIONS

EVERY BARTENDER AND LOUNGE LIZARD SHOULD KNOW HOW TO ANSWER

Robert Plotkin

BarMedia
Tucson, Arizona
2005

OTHER BOOKS BY ROBERT PLOTKIN

Beverage Operator's Survival Guide (2005)
The Original Guide to American Cocktails and Drinks – 5th Edition (2004)
The Original Pocket Guide to American Cocktails and Drinks (2004)
The Professional Bartender's Training Manual - 3rd Edition (2002)
Drinks For All Ages – The Original Guide to Alcohol-Free Beverages and Drinks (2002)
Caribe Rum – The Original Guide to Caribbean Rum and Drinks (2001)
Successful Beverage Management – Proven Strategies for the On-Premise Operator (2000)
¡Toma! Margaritas! The Original Guide to Margaritas and Tequila (1999)
Preventing Internal Theft: A Bar Owner's Guide - 2nd Edition (1998)
Increasing Bar Sales – Creative Twists to Bigger Profits (1997)
Reducing Bar Costs: A Survival Guide for the '90s (1993)
501 Questions Every Bartender Should Know How to Answer (1993)
The Professional Guide to Bartending: The Encyclopedia of American Mixology (1991)
The Intervention Handbook: The Legal Aspects of Serving Alcohol - 2nd Edition (1990)

Book Design
Dave Lazarus
Katie Alter

ISBN 0-945562-32-2

Publisher

BarMedia
P. O. Box 14486
Tucson, Arizona   85732-4486
520.747.8131
www.barmedia.com

TABLE OF CONTENTS

Introduction

Introduction

What will club soda poured into an empty glass reveal about the glass? Why does vodka have a neutral flavor? What is the difference between a top-fermenting and bottom-fermenting beer? What is Solera aging? Which side of the lemon twist faces the glass before twisting?

These are questions everyone making their livelihood behind a bar, or who are proud to call themselves lounge lizards should know how to answer.

Such is the working premise behind this book. Its 1001 questions will test your knowledge of liquors, liqueurs, beers, wines, alcohol-awareness and professional mixology. Whether you're a rookie bartender, seasoned pro, or devoted fan, this one-of-a-kind book is guaranteed to challenge and expand your expertise.

This material is also an invaluable training resource. It presents a unique opportunity to learn what a bartending staff knows about their chosen field of endeavor. Included in the book are three bartending exams, graduated in difficulty and ready to use for on-premise training. The tests can also be used to make the considerable task of determining a bartending applicant's level of expertise and quantifying his or her work experience more reliable.

The material in *1001 Questions Every Bartender and Lounge Lizard Should Know How To Answer* is divided into the following five sections:

• Product Knowledge: Liquors, Liqueurs, Beers and Wines

• Professional Mixology: The Who, What, Where, When and Why of Bartending

• What's Your Alcohol I.Q.?

• Questions for Seasoned Pros

• Bar Exams: Entry Level, Intermediate and Advanced

The answer keys to the questions and sample bartending tests can be found in the sixth section.

So enjoy, learn something and have fun.

Robert Plotkin
BarMedia
Tucson, Arizona

SECTION 1
PRODUCT KNOWLEDGE

Liquors, Liqueurs, Beers and Wines

What
first London
majority of the
are distilled from what
the Bacardi Rum distillery
Puerto Rico? What is the primary
nale Amaretto? Where is Seagram's 7
How does the pear get into the bottle of
acknowledged as the first 100% blue agave
almond-flavored liqueurs derive their flavor?
century alchemists in Europe as a medicinal
and Pernod turns these liqueurs cloudy
What whisky was introduced in 1939 to
King George and Queen Elizabeth to
nearly all brands of gin? With regards to
What is the technical difference between
character difference between lagers and
sling cocktail, a drink originated at a London
best-selling brand of Goldwasser? The
purportedly brought to Scotland by Bonnie
whisky-based liqueur is made on the Isle of
the first to be marketed in a square-shaped
Black Label or White Label Bourbon? What
essence? What product is most closely
does sherry originally come from? Baileys
coffee, cream and what distilled spirit? What
Chambord Royale Liqueur has the rich
what is the principle
Curaçao

was the
Dry Gin? The
world's vodkas
product? Where was
located before it moved to
flavor of famed Disaronno Origi-
Crown Blended Whiskey produced?
Poire William Eau-de-vie? What brand is
tequila imported into the U.S.? How do
What liqueur was formulated by 16th
elixir? What ingredient in sambuca, ouzo
when poured over ice or mixed with water?
commemorate the unprecedented visit of
Canada? What is the primary botanical in
the distilling of gin, what are botanicals?
lagers and ales? What is the principle
ales? What liqueur is actually a bottled gin
restaurant in the late 1800s? What is the
recipe for what renowned liqueur was
Prince Charlie in 1745? What famous Scotch
Skye? What famous American whiskey was
bottle? Which is aged longer, Wild Turkey
famous Russian vodka is infused with lemon
associated with solera aging? What country
Original Irish Cream is made from chocolate,
liqueur bears the initials D.O.M. on its label?
flavor of what fruit? Other than color,
difference between Blue
and Triple

1. What was the first London Dry Gin?

2. The majority of the world's vodkas are distilled from what product?

3. This renowned small-batch, 120-proof-plus bourbon is bottled undiluted and unfiltered; essentially straight from the barrel?

4. Where was the Bacardi Rum distillery located before it moved to Puerto Rico?

5. What is the primary flavor of famed Disaronno Originale Amaretto?

6. This smoky, Mexican spirit is perhaps best known for the "little something extra" added to each bottle.

7. What is Disaronno Originale Amaretto?

8. Made in Perth, Scotland since the 1860s, this blend has the distinction of being the first bottled Scotch whisky.

9. This company boasts of being the oldest whiskey distillery in the world.

10. Where is Seagram's 7 Crown Blended Whiskey produced?

11. How does the pear get into the bottle of Poire William Eau-de-vie?

12. What brand is acknowledged as the first 100% blue agave tequila imported into the U.S.?

13. How do almond-flavored liqueurs derive their flavor?

14. This famous Mexican liqueur is made from coffee beans and cane spirits.

15. What liqueur was formulated by 16th century alchemists in Europe as a medicinal elixir?

16. Made from a blend of Caribbean rums on the island of Tortola, this full-bodied spirit was standard issue for sailors of the British Royal Navy from 1655 until 1970.

17. What ingredient in sambuca, ouzo and Pernod turns these liqueurs cloudy when poured over ice or mixed with water?

18. This brand is the best selling single malt Scotch whisky in Scotland.

19. What whisky was introduced in 1939 to commemorate the unprecedented visit of King George and Queen Elizabeth to Canada?

20. What is the primary botanical in nearly all brands of gin?

21. With regards to the distilling of gin, what are botanicals?

22. What is the technical difference between lagers and ales?

23. What is the principle character difference between lagers and ales?

24. What liqueur is actually a bottled gin sling cocktail, a drink originated at a London restaurant in the late 1800s?

25. This famous Italian liqueur is thought to have been formulated as a love potion by a coven of witches?

26. What is the best-selling brand of Goldwasser?

27. This 100 proof schnapps is made in the Black Forest of Bavaria.

28. The recipe for what renowned liqueur was purportedly brought to Scotland by Bonnie Prince Charlie in 1745?

29. What famous Scotch whisky-based liqueur is made on the Isle of Skye?

30. Drier and more potent than anisette, this semi-sweet anise liqueur is made in Greece and Cyprus.

31. What famous American whiskey was the first to be marketed in a square-shaped bottle?

32. This 6-year-old Canadian whisky has been made by Hiram Walker in Ontario since the late 1800s.

33. Which is aged longer, Wild Turkey Black Label or White Label Bourbon?

34. This world famous Russian vodka is distilled in Moscow from winter wheat .

35. What famous Russian vodka is infused with lemon essence?

36. This award-winning Russian vodka is quadruple distilled from winter wheat and glacier water.

37. What product is most closely associated with solera aging?

38. What country does sherry originally come from?

39. Baileys Original Irish Cream is made from chocolate, coffee, cream and what distilled spirit?

40. What liqueur bears the initials D.O.M. on its label?

41. Chambord Royale Liqueur has the rich flavor of what fruit?

42. Other than color, what is the principle difference between Blue Curaçao and Triple Sec?

43. This liqueur is made from black currants grown principally in the Burgundy region of France.

44. What is America's first proprietary liqueur?

45. What infamous liqueur was dubbed the "Green Muse?"

BRUSHING UP ON YOUR PRODUCT KNOWLEDGE

One of the things that goes along with being a bartender is being barraged by questions from the curious and pondering. Guests staring at the back bar or watching drinks being made are often prompted to inquire, "What is that?" or "What's the difference between…?" or "Do you happen to know…?"

Another thing that goes with the territory is the need to be informed enough to answer those questions. To that end, we've devised this little quiz to test your knowledge of many of the spirits on your back bar. Pair up each spirit with the definition of what it is.

1. Armagnac

2. Brandy de Jerez

3. Caçacha

4. Calvados

5. Eau-de-vie

6. Grappa

7. Jenever

8. Kirschwasser

9. Mead

10. Ouzo

11. Pineau des Charentes

12. Poire William

13. Ricard

14. Sambuca

15. Slivovitz

A. An eau-de-vie distilled from cherries

B. A Greek liqueur flavored with anise

C. A South American spirit distilled from sugar cane

D. Either a young or unaged brandy

E. An anise liqueur; a type of pastis

F. An eau-de-vie made from pears

G. A high-proof, Hungarian plum brandy

H. A brandy made from the remnants of winemaking

I. A brandy made in and around Gascony, France

J. A wine fortified with cognac

K. A French apple brandy made in Normandy

L. A liqueur flavored with elderberry berries

M. A brandy made in the south of Spain

N. A wine made from heather or clover honey

O. A type of gin distilled in Holland

1.-I 2.-M 3.-C 4.-K 5.-D 6.-H 7.-O 8.-A 9.-N 10.-B 11.-J 12.-F 13.-E 14.-L 15.-G

46. What popular Scandinavian spirit is twice-distilled from either grain or potatoes and has the flavor of caraway?

47. Metaxa 5 and 7 Star brandies are produced in what nation?

48. This brandy is made in pot stills and aged in new Limousin oak casks.

49. Made from fermented sugar cane molasses in column stills, this is the world's best selling type of rum.

50. Brewed with bottom-fermenting yeasts, it is the most widely produced type of beer in America.

51. This highly popular, German liqueur is made from an infusion of 56 herbs, roots, fruit and gentian.

52. What is the principal difference between a brandy and an eau de vie?

53. What spirit can be distilled from grain, potatoes, rice, sugar beets, or grapes?

54. This Puerto Rican rum is flavored with a blend of clove, allspice and cinnamon.

55. One of the most popular whiskies in the world, it has been blended in Aberdeen, Scotland, in a 12-, 18- and 21-year-old version.

56. What type of whisky is Chivas Regal?

57. What do the initials "V.O." on the label of Seagram's Canadian whisky stand for?

58. What liquor is compounded by redistilling neutral grain spirits with berries, roots, bark, seeds and plant parts?

59. This spirit bears the name of the brand's Russian founder who was considered the "Purveyor of Vodka to the Czars."

60. This Bushmills single malt whiskey is triple-distilled in a copper pot still and aged 9 to 11 years in used sherry oak casks.

61. This famous Scotch whisky was the first to be blended specifically for American tastes.

62. What is rum distilled from?

63. This brand of rum has been distilled in Kingston, Jamaica, since 1879.

64. What are most brandies distilled from?

65. What is Akvavit (Aquavit) made from?

WHAT'S ALL THE BROUHAHA ABOUT BEER?

Archie Bunker maintained that you don't buy beer, you just rent it for a while. Well, a lot of Americans must be renting these days. Beer remains the favorite alcoholic beverage of men and the second most frequent request of women. Yet despite its enormous popularity, there is a lot about beer you might not know.

1. What will happen when dust, dirt or salt are dropped into a glass of beer?
2. What styles of beer are produced in an alembic still?
3. What will prolonged exposure to fluorescent light do to beer?
4. Why are there no bubbles visible in a capped bottle of beer?
5. What will happen to draft beer if it is dispensed at too high of a pressure?
6. What will happen if it is dispensed at too low of a pressure?
7. What will happen to draft beer if it is dispensed at too low of a temperature?
8. What will happen if it is dispensed at too high of a temperature?
9. What is a lager?
10. What is ale?
11. What is Belgium (Brussels) lace?
12. What brewery first marketed "dry" beer?
13. What are the basic components of most beer?
14. What is "ice" beer?
15. What are hops?
16. What role does yeast play in the production of beer?
17. What is barley malt?
18. What is "krausening?"
19. What characteristics do you look for in the head of a well-made beer?
20. What is a Lambic beer?

Answers on page 106.

66. Made from fermented honey, herbs and water, it was the potable of preference of Friar Tuck, Little John and Robin Hood.

67. What liqueur is the modern version of Absinthe, only now made without toxic wormwood?

68. This Italian, anise-flavored liqueur is actually made from wild Elderbush berries.

69. What famous liqueur is made with a base of Fine Champagne cognac and a blend of exotic bitter and sweet oranges?

70. This famous liqueur was released to commemorate the 150th anniversary of Marnier-Lapostolle.

71. This classic French liqueur was originally labeled "Triple Sec White Curaçao" and is now know by the name of its creator.

72. Originally brewed in Czechoslovakia, it is a bottom-fermented beer, typically golden-colored, dry and crisp; it is the most widely imitated style of beer.

73. This famous flavored rum is made from a blend of natural coconut flavorings and Jamaican light rum.

74. This aromatic liqueur is made in Nassau, Bahamas, from herbs, spices, vanilla and light rum.

75. This almond-flavored cordial obtains its flavor from crushed apricot and peach pits.

76. What is the alcohol-base of Drambuie?

77. The House of Burrough has produced this famous London Dry Gin since the early 1800s.

78. Established in 1804, this Jamaican firm produces one of the most famous brands of Demerara rum.

79. Made in Normandy, France, this brandy is distilled from cider apples and is aged in oak casks prior to bottling.

80. Why are the islands in the Caribbean basin renowned for producing rum?

81. Are most Scotch whiskies blended or straight?

82. What type of charcoal is used to filter Jack Daniel's Tennessee Whiskey?

83. First distilled in the 1830s by Scottish immigrants, this category of whisky is typically made from a blend of rye, corn and barley whiskies.

84. What label of rum is marketed as the "Planter's Punch Brand?"

85. What do Stolichnaya Citros and Absolut Citron have in common?

Rum without question is the most popular spirit in the world. Every bar in the country carries it in their well and several brands on their back bar. Now is the time to capitalize on rum's nearly universal appeal. You stand to reap tremendous returns if you do.

Rum is extremely versatile, equaling vodka in that respect. But unlike vodka, rum has an irresistible taste and a savory aroma that lifts it head and shoulders above any other light liquor. Equally important, rum is fun and enjoyable. It has a carefree reputation that few other products enjoy. So jump in with both feet and catch a rum state of mind.

But first, you have to know who the players are. To that end, we've created a little trivia challenge that will test your Rum/Rhum IQ.

1. Appleton Estate Extra	A. Guyana
2. Rhum Barbancourt Réserve Spéciale	B. Saint Vincent
3. Bacardi Carta Blanca	C. Jamaica
4. Mount Gay Eclipse	D. Bermuda
5. Pyrat Planter's Gold X.O.	E. Antilles
6. Cruzan Single Barrel	F. Trinidad
7. Angostura 1824	G. Barbados
8. Conch Republic Black	H. Dominican Republic
9. Gosling's Black Seal	I. Cuba
10. Whaler's Vanille	J. Yucatan
11. El Dorado 15-year	K. Costa Rica
12. Cohiba Black	L. Tortola
13. D'Aristi Añejo Special	M. Haiti
14. Havana Club Añejo Reserva	N. Florida
15. Westerhall Plantation	O. Puerto Rico
16. Kaniche	P. US Virgin Islands
17. Mangoustan's Rhum	Q. Queensland, Australia
18. Sunset Light	R. Anguilla
19. Pusser's Blue Label	S. Hawaii
20. Gran Blasón Añejo	T. Guatemala
21. Montecristo 12-year	U. Grenada
22. Stubb's Light	V. Guadeloupe

1.-C 2.-M 3.-O 4.-G 5.-R 6.-P 7.-F 8.-N 9.-D 10.-S 11.-A 12.-H 13.-J 14.-I 15.-U 16.-V 17.-E 18.-B 19.-L 20.-K 21.-T 22.-Q

86. Bourbon is distilled primarily from what grain?

87. Which is usually darker, bourbon or Scotch?

88. Made with top-fermenting yeasts, this type of brew is typically heavy-bodied, copper-colored (or darker), high in alcohol and most closely identified with English-style beers.

89. Most closely associated with Italy, this sweet, fortified aperitif is infused with herbs, roots, seeds, quinine and various other botanicals.

90. What gives red wine the color lacking in white wine?

91. Which of the basic liquors is usually poured at the highest proof?

92. Is schnapps a liquor or liqueur?

93. What is Boodles?

94. Why does vodka have a neutral flavor?

95. More than 50 distilled spirits comprise the blend of this classic brand of American whiskey.

96. This distillery has been producing bourbon in Clermont, Kentucky since 1795.

97. How do many Canadians refer to their indigenous whisky?

98. Tia Maria is a liqueur made from Blue Mountain coffee beans and a base of what distilled spirit?

99. What classic American liqueur is made from a base of neutral spirits and flavored with peach liqueur, fresh peaches and citrus extracts?

100. This classic American liqueur is often mistaken as a bourbon.

101. What bitters is made in Port-of-Spain, Trinidad?

102. What product became one of the former Soviet Union's most successful exports to the West?

103. What invaluable contribution to the production of bourbon is Reverend Elijah Craig credited with?

104. What is a single malt Scotch whisky?

105. What is the primary difference between Chivas Regal and Glenfiddich?

106. What type of spirit is obtained by distilling fermented molasses or fresh sugar cane juice?

107. What is an eau de vie?

108. This type of rum contains a minimum of 57.14% alcohol by volume.

WHAT'S YOUR TEQUILA IQ?

In Mexico, it is referred to as *Tequila Puro*. In the United States, we know them as 100% agave tequilas. They have captivated the imagination of the American drinking public, making them the fastest growing category of spirits in the country. Interest in tequila has been nothing short of phenomenal.

The proliferation of brands of tequila, however, has left many consumers feeling overwhelmed. Increasingly more people are asking us what's the difference between the various tequilas. If they're made from nothing but agave, then how can there be such a huge disparity between quality, taste and selling price?

Premium, 100% agave tequilas are single-ingredient products. They essentially contain nothing but blue agave and a fractional amount of demineralized water. Their inherent differences have to do with the techniques and process by which they are made.

The following has been devised to test your tequila IQ. Salud!

1. What is only one variety of agave that tequila can legally be produced from?
2. Why are the agaves not harvested until the plants reach their optimum maturity?
3. Why is a harvested agave referred to as a *piña*?
4. After the agaves are crushed at the distillery, why are they loaded into a hornos?
5. What happens to the juice—called *aguamiel*—after it is extracted from the baked agaves?
6. What happens during fermentation?
7. What happens to the juice after fermentation?
8. According to Mexican law, how many times must tequila be distilled?
9. What is reposado tequila?
10. What is añejo tequila?
11. What is El Tesoro Paradiso Añejo?
12. What is Del Dueño Jerezito Añejo?
13. What is a *mixto* tequila?
14. What is XXX Siglo Treinta?
15. What is an *hornos*?

Answers on page 106.

109. This famed, full-bodied brandy is made in the French province of Gascony.

110. What is the primary difference between a V.S. and a V.S.O.P. Cognac?

111. What is added to Benedictine D.O.M. to make the liqueur B. & B.?

112. Produced since 1607 by Carthusian monks, this French liqueur is made from brandy, wild mountain herbs and redistilled four times before aging.

113. This Italian black sambuca is made from anise, elderflower and lemon.

114. What does Liquore Galliano taste like?

115. This liqueur is known as Cuarenta y Tres in its homeland of Spain.

116. How is gin infused with its taste and aroma?

117. By the 1917 overthrow of the Czar, this Russian company was producing an extraordinary one million liters of vodka a day.

118. Old Overholt is an example of what type of American whiskey?

119. Crown Royal is a super-premium label of what type of whiskey?

120. In what state is the Ezra Brooks distillery located?

121. To what product did Mr. Justerini and Mr. Brooks lend their names?

122. What whisky bears the name of a famous 1870s clipper ship?

123. What type of whisky is distilled entirely from malted barley?

124. In what Scotch-producing region will you find The Glenlivet Distillery?

125. What is Demerara rum?

126. What is Poire William?

127. What are pomace brandies?

128. What is the difference between a "split" and "half-bottle" of wine?

129. This French aperitif wine is produced in both a "Blanc" and "Rouge" version and is fortified to 19% abv.

130. This term is used to describe the thickness or consistency of a beer as perceived in the mouth.

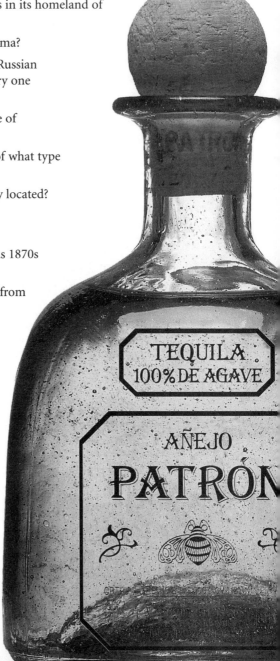

TEQUILA
100% DE AGAVE

AÑEJO

PATRÓN

WHERE DOES THIS LABEL OF BEER COME FROM?

Beer is one of the world's most widely produced and widely consumed alcoholic potables. It is a relatively simple substance — the basic components of most are barley, hops, yeast and water.

We are all very much a product of our environment. The same holds true for beer. Let's see what you know about where the world's great beers hail from by matching the following labels of beers with their country of origin:

1. Aass	A. Austria
2. Amstel	B. Australia
3. Bank's Ebony	C. Barbados
4. Beamish Stout	D. Belgium
5. Blitz-Weinhard	E. Brazil
6. Boon Rawd	F. Canada
7. Brahma	G. China
8. Brain	H. Czech Republic
9. Braü AG	I. Denmark
10. Carib Lager	J. France
11. Carling O'Keefe	K. Holland
12. Carlsberg Elephant	L. Ireland
13. Cisk Lager	M. Jamaica
14. Lindemans Kriek	N. Malta
15. Lion Lager	O. Mexico
16. Löwenbraü	P. Norway
17. Negra Modelo	Q. Philippines
18. Ngok' Biere	R. Republic of Congo
19. Pelforth Pale	S. Singapore
20. Pilsner Urquell	T. Sri Lanka
21. Red Stripe Lager	U. Switzerland
22. San Miguel	V. Thailand
23. Singha Lager	W. Trinidad
24. Tooth's Sheaf Stout	X. United Kingdom
25. Tsingtao	Y. United States

1.-P 2.-K 3.-C 4.-L 5.-Y 6.-V 7.-E 8.-X 9.-A 10.-W 11.-I 12.-F 13.-N 14.-D 15.-T 16.-U 17.-O 18.-R 19.-J 20.-H 21.-M 22.-Q 23.-S 24.-B 25.-G

131. This aromatic spirit is distilled principally in Scandinavian countries from grain, caraway seeds and occasionally other botanicals.

132. Aquavit and Akvavit are different spellings for what popular Scandinavian spirit?

133. This clear, spicy mint liqueur is lighter and drier than creme de menthe.

134. This dry, aromatic liqueur is made in Europe from cumin, caraway and neutral grain spirits.

135. This classic Italian liqueur is made in the Piedmont region from woodland herbs, berries and hazelnuts.

136. What is the French designation for crème de almond?

137. Other than color, what is the principle difference between what and dark crème de cacao?

138. Is Southern Comfort a liquor or liqueur?

139. What, if any any, are the differences between Johnnie Walker Red Label and Black Label?

140. This type of Dutch juniper-infused spirit is the predecessor of London Dry Gin.

141. Whose portrait appears on the Bombay Gin label?

142. Wyborowa Vodka is imported from what country?

143. What is Stolichnaya Pertsovka?

144. What color are whiskies when they come out of the still?

145. How long is Wild Turkey 101 proof bourbon aged in wood?

146. This famous 12-year-old blended Scotch whisky is produced by Haig & Haig.

147. This company has the distinction of operating Scotland's first legally registered distillery.

148. Chivas Regal issued this 21-year-old blended Scotch whisky in honor of Queen Elizabeth's 1953 coronation.

1. Appleton Estate		A.	Dutch Dry Gin
2. Asbach Uralt		B.	Irish Single Malt
3. Auchentoshan		C.	Orkney Single Malt
4. Belvedere		D.	Small Batch Bourbon
5. Blanton's		E.	American Potato Vodka
6. Boodles		F.	Kentucky Bourbon
7. Chopin		G.	Haitian Rum
8. de Fussigny		H.	Campbeltown Single Malt
9. de Montal		I.	German Brandy
10. El Tesoro		J.	Canadian Blended Whisky
11. Gentleman Jack		K.	Russian Wheat Vodka
12. Germain-Robin		L.	American Blended Whiskey
13. Glenmorangie		M.	Naval Rum
14. Gooderham & Worts		N.	Barbados Rum
15. Knob Creek		O.	Polish Rye Vodka
16. Lagavulin		P.	Jamaican Rum
17. Leyden		Q.	London Dry Gin
18. Macallan		R.	Armagnac
19. Maker's Mark		S.	Single Barrel Bourbon
20. Mount Gay		T.	Islay Single Malt
21. Pusser's		U.	American Alambic Brandy
22. Rhum Barbancourt		V.	Isle of Skye Single Malt
23. Scapa		W.	Small Batch Canadian Whisky
24. Seagram's 7		X.	Highland Single Malt
25. Seagram's VO		Y.	Speyside Highland Single Malt
26. Springbank		Z.	Cognac
27. Stolichnaya Gold		AA.	100% Blue Agave Tequila
28. Talisker		BB.	Lowland Single Malt
29. Teton Glacier		CC.	Polish Potato Vodka
30. Tyrconnell		DD.	Tennessee Whiskey

1.-P 2.-I 3.-BB 4.-O 5.-S 6.-Q 7.-CC 8.-Z 9.-R 10.-AA 11.-DD 12.-U 13.-X 14.-W 15.-D 16.-T 17.-A 18.-Y 19.-F 20.-N 21.-M 22.-G 23.-C 24.-L 25.-J 26.-H 27.-K 28.-V 29.-E 30.-B

Product Knowledge   15

149. This 2-year-old, blended amber rum is made from fermented sugar cane molasses in Bridgetown, Barbados.

150. What do grappa and marc have in common?

151. What is armagnac?

152. What is tequila distilled from?

153. This Italian aromatic liqueur is made from an infusion of bitter herbs and popularly mixed with club soda.

154. Produced in Jamaica since the late 1700s, this liqueur is lighter and drier than Kahlúa.

155. Della Norte is the black version of this brand of sambuca.

156. What is the predominant flavor of Pernod?

157. What is Pernod?

158. This liqueur was first produced in 1525 as an offering of love in Saronno, Italy?

159. Slightly sweeter than Triple Sec, this liqueur is made from the peels of oranges grown in the Dutch West Indies.

160. What famous American liqueur was originally marketed in 1875 in New Orleans as "Cuff and Buttons?"

161. This liqueur is made from oranges, herbs and premium Canadian whisky.

162. What is Irish Mist?

163. The oil of essence of peppermint is used to produce what cordial?

164. This popular French liqueur is made from small black raspberries, herbs and honey.

165. The name of this Japanese, honeydew-flavored liqueur literally means "green."

166. What is the American version of prunelle?

167. This French monastery liqueur is made by the Carthusian monks from an infusion of brandy and 130 wild mountain herbs.

168. This French monastery liqueur is slightly sweeter and less aromatic than the more famous green version.

169. This amber, hoppy brew is considered a hybrid, being made from both top- and bottom-fermenting yeasts; it is made only in San Francisco.

170. This Dutch chocolate-mint liqueur has been made in Holland since the 1500s.

HEY, WHERE'S THAT COME FROM?

Everyone and everything hails from somewhere. You know where you come from, but what about the products on your back bar. You handle them everyday, but do you even know their hometowns?

Let's take a quick check of how familiar you are with where these famous products come from, shall we? Match each spirit with its city of origin.

1. Bacardi Reserve	A. Aberdeen, Scotland
2. Beefeater Gin	B. Bardstown, KY
3. Blanton's Bourbon	C. Berlin, Germany
4. Chivas Regal Royal Salute Blended Scotch	D. Bridgetown, Barbados
5. Courvoisier VSOP Cognac	E. Dublin, Ireland
6. Crown Royal Canadian Whisky	F. Finsbury England
7. Dewar's White Label Blended Scotch	G. Jarnac, France
8. Germain-Robin Brandy	H. Lawrenceburg, IN
9. Jägermeister	I. Lawrenceburg, KY
10. Jameson 1780 Whiskey	J. London, England
11. Ketel One Vodka	K. Moscow, Russia
12. Martini & Rossi Vermouth	L. Perth, Scotland
13. Mount Gay Eclipse Rum	M. San Juan, Puerto Rico
14. Original Cristall Vodka	N. Schiedam, Holland
15. Seagram's Seven Whiskey	O. Tallinn, Estonia
16. Tanqueray Gin	P. Torino, Italy
17. Türi Vodka	Q. Ukiah, California
18. Wild Turkey Bourbon	R. Warsaw, Poland
19. Wodka Gorbatschow	S. Waterloo, Ontario
20. Wyborowa Vodka	T. Wolfenbüttel, Germany

1.-M 2.-J 3.-B 4.-A 5.-G 6.-S 7.-L 8.-Q 9.-T 10.-E 11.-N 12.-P 13.-D
14.-K 15.-H 16.-F 17.-O 18.-I 19.-C 20.-R

171. This dry, menthol-flavored schnapps is imported from Canada.

172. This Spanish liqueur is made from vanilla, citrus, milk and 43 different herbs.

173. This American liqueur is named after a world famous maker of chocolate.

174. What Rumple Minze?

175. What is Bäerenjäeger?

176. This beer is a potent, full-bodied, bottom-fermented brew with origins in Einbeck, Germany.

177. What is Fernet Branca?

178. Most closely associated with France, this aperitif wine is aged 2-3 years in oak casks exposed to the elements to accelerate maturation.

179. This highly sought-after French red wine is bottled extremely young and cannot be legally sold before the third Thursday in November.

180. This famous New Orleans bitters has a pronounced anise flavor.

181. What happens to tequila when it is aged in wood?

182. The Grande Champagne district can be found in what famous brandy producing region of France?

183. What is Slivovitz?

184. The name of this colorless, unaged brandy translates to the "water of life?"

185. What is an "over proof" rum?

186. What is the name of Stolichnaya's lemon-infused vodka?

187. What brand of gin is most closely associated with the British Royal Navy?

188. This dry, white rum from Queensland, Australia, is distilled from fermented sugar cane molasses.

189. What gives many Scotch whiskies their singularly smoky flavor?

190. This whisky has the distinction of being the first commercially blended Scotch.

191. George Washington distilled this famous brand of straight whiskey.

192. This whiskey lays claim to being the first sour mash bourbon.

OUR MATCH GAME OF THE SPIRITS II

Day after day they sit patiently on your back bar. You use them everyday, they make you a lot of money, you may even consider many of them your close friends, but are you quite positive you know what they are? They have a life too, so to speak.

Let's take a quick check of your f/q (familiarity quotient) of what these famous products are, shall we? Match each spirit with what it is.

1. A. Hardy Noces d'Or	A. French triple-distilled gin
2. Auchentoshan	B. French pure-grain vodka
3. Century of Malts	C. 6-year old bourbon whiskey
4. Chinaco	D. Ukrainian chocolate flavored vodka
5. Citadelle	E. Small batch, 8-year old bourbon
6. Connemara	F. American apple brandy
7. Dalmore Cigar Malt	G. Swedish small-batch grain vodka
8. Germain-Robin Perfection	H. Martinique agricole rum
9. Goldenbarr	I. Single malt whiskey made in Oregon
10. Grey Goose	J. Single Campbeltown malt whisky
11. Highland Park	K. Single Highland malt Scotch whisky
12. Jefferson's Reserve	L. Blended Scotch whisky by Chivas Regal
13. Krolewska	
14. Lagavulin	M. English pot-distilled gin
15. Laird's	N. Polish wheat vodka
16. Lammerlaw	O. Haitian rum aged in Limousin oak
17. Level	P. Single Orkney malt Scotch whisky
18. McCarthy's Whiskey	Q. Single Islay malt Scotch whisky
19. Mezzaluna	R. Single Lowlands malt Scotch whisky
20. Old Montana Red Eye	S. 100% Blue Agave Tequila
21. Plymouth	T. New Zealand single malt whisky
22. Rhum Barbancourt	U. American alambic brandy
23. Rhum Saint James	V. Irish single malt whiskey
24. Springbank	W. Italian pure-grain vodka
25. Tangle Ridge	X. Triple-distilled Dutch vodka
26. Van Gogh	Y. 10-year Canadian whisky
	Z. Grande Champagne cognac

1.-Z 2.-R 3.-L 4.-S 5.-A 6.-V 7.-K 8.-U 9.-D 10.-B 11.-P 12.-E 13.-N 14.-Q 15.-F 16.-T 17.-G 18.-I 19.-W 20.-C 21.-M 22.-O 23.-H 24.-J 25.-Y 26.-X

193. This Swedish vodka is infused with paprika and jalapeño pepper.

194. What Swedish vodka is infused with citrus?

195. This famous American whiskey lays claim to being the first bourbon sold in a bottle.

196. This vodka is made in Belgium and distilled entirely from sugar beets.

197. Made in Frankfort, Kentucky, this whiskey is considered the first single cask bourbon.

198. This famous brand of Irish whiskey was originally distilled in Dublin in 1780 and is now made at the renowned Midleton Distillery.

199. This handcrafted whiskey is the first new product released by Jack Daniel's in 100 years.

200. Talisker is made in what whisky-producing region of Scotland?

201. In the early 1900s, this blended Scotch was named the official whisky of the House of Commons.

202. This famous dark, aromatic rhum is double distilled on the island of Haiti from sugar cane juice.

203. What is Laird's Applejack?

204. By law, tequila must contain a minimum of 51% agave, what constitutes the remaining 49 percent?

205. What is grappa?

206. What is Sherry?

207. Produced in both a sweet and a dry, bitter (Irish) version, this style of beer is typically full-bodied, dark in color and brewed using roasted, unmalted barley.

208. What is framboise?

209. This clear, orange liqueur is lighter and drier than Curaçao.

210. What is the difference between green and white crème de menthe?

211. This bottled neutral grain spirits is 95% alcohol by volume.

212. Released in 1977, this liqueur is made on a base of Grande Champagne cognacs ranging in age up to 50 years.

213. Produced since 1818, this aged, Danish cherry liqueur is named after its founder.

214. Made by the Lapostelle family, this French liqueur is made from brandy and Dalmatian cherries.

215. This Belgian liqueur is made from Andalusian tangerines and well aged cognac.

EXPLORING THE WIDE WORLD OF LIQUEURS

Try to imagine operating a busy bar without liqueurs. You wouldn't be busy for long without products such as Kahlúa, Baileys Irish Cream or triple sec. Consider what your business would be like with no Disaronno Amaretto or Grand Marnier. With few exceptions, liqueurs are the essential flavor components behind most great cocktails and specialty drinks.

Today, most liqueurs are produced to be lighter and drier, more in step with contemporary tastes. The classic proprietary liqueurs owe their longevity to the fact that they're well balanced and fabulously delicious.

So, what's your liqueur IQ these days? Not sure? Well, we've devised this little quiz to help you find out.

1. Baileys	A. Jamaican coffee and chocolate liqueur
2. Chambord	B. French liqueur made with oranges and cognac
3. Cointreau	C. Italian liqueur made from elderbush berries
4. Disaronno Amaretto	D. French black raspberry liqueur
5. Drambuie	E. Japanese liqueur with a honeydew flavor
6. Frangelico	F. Italian liqueur with a pronounced anise flavor
7. Godiva	G. Proprietary Italian liqueur with an almond flavor
8. Grand Marnier	H. Italian liqueur made from hazelnuts and brandy
9. Irish Mist	I. Irish liqueur made from whiskey and herbs
10. Jägermeister	J. German liqueur made from a blend of 56 spices
11. Kahlúa	K Semi-sweet anise liqueur made in Greece
12. Licor 43	L. Spanish liqueur made from brandy, fruit and herbs
13. Liquore Galliano	M. Semi-sweet chocolate liqueur made in New York
14. Midori	N. Scotch-based liqueur flavored with heather honey
15. Ouzo	O. Aromatic orange liqueur made in France
16. Sambuca	P. American liqueur produced with peach extracts
17. Southern Comfort	Q. Mexican liqueur flavored with coffee beans
18. Strega	R. Italian liqueur made from 70 herbs and citrus
19. Tia Maria	S. Italian liqueur made with herbs and brandy
20. Tuaca	T. Cream liqueur made with Ireland whiskey

1.-T 2.-D 3.-O 4.-G 5.-N 6.-H 7.-M 8.-B 9.-I 10.-J 11.-Q 12.-L 13.-F 14.-E 15.-K 16.-C 17.-P 18.-R 19.-A 20.-S

216. This clear, aromatic liqueur is made from almonds and Dalmation Marasca cherries.

217. Made from a 500-year-old recipe, this Italian semi-sweet liqueur is made from brandy, herbs and fruit.

218. This is a BATF classification for an American lager with an alcohol content of 5% to 7.5% by volume.

219. This renowned cognac house is perhaps best known for their Louis XIII brandy.

220. Made in France since 1872, this French fortified aperitif is semi-dry and has the subtle flavor of oranges, herbs and quinine.

221. This colorful tropical concoction originated at the Zanzibar Club in London.

222. This type of gin in made in either a "Jonge" or "Oude" style?

223. This super-premium, 94 proof London Dry Gin is made with 10 botanicals and aromatics and is the product of a singular distillation process.

224. This famous London Dry Gin is distilled in Finsbury, England, which was the site of a renowned health spa known for the purity of its water.

225. This 86 proof, London Dry Gin is still made according to its original 1761 formula.

226. A Fine Champagne cognac is made from a blend of brandies from what two regions?

227. This Swedish vodka is flavored with European black currants.

228. This triple-distilled, 12 year old superpremium Irish whiskey is aged in oak casks previously used to age sherry and is named for its founder.

229. The name of this famous Highland single malt Scotch whisky means "Valley of the Deer."

230. This famous 100% agave reposado tequila is aged 3-6 months in large oak vats and produced under the Sauza label.

231. What eau de vie is traditionally sold with a pear in the bottle?

232. What is Kirsch?

233. Made according to a recipe dating back to the 1700's, this superpremium Bombay gin is the product of a unique distillation process.

234. On what island is the medium-bodied rum Cockspur distilled?

235. Founded in 1715, this famous cognac house is best known for their Cordon Bleu and Cordon Argent brandies.

236. This brand of Akvavit has been made in Denmark since 1846 from neutral grain spirits and caraway.

237. This dry, aromatic eau de vie is made from the fermented mash of William, Bartlett and Anjou pears.

238. The name Napoleon is associated with what type of spirit?

239. Very Superior (or Special) Old Pale is often found as a designation on what type of spirit?

240. What do the initials "C.C." stand for a famous label of whisky?

241. What is an agricole rum?

242. What is a mixto tequila?

243. What is tequila?

244. What is brandy?

245. What is rum?

246. Heaven Hill Distillery makes what is considered the first vintage dated, single barrel bourbon.

247. What is the world's best known framboise?

248. What is Bärenjäger?

249. What is Jägermeister?

250. What is applejack?

251. This English gin is distilled with the fewest number of botanicals and is intended to appeal to vodka drinkers.

252. Made at the Dirkzwager Distillery in Schiedam, Holland, this vodka is infused with the tangy, fermented juice of organic, tree-ripened apples.

253. Made by Sauza, this silver tequila is triple-distilled in an alembic still and bottled within 24 hours of distillation.

254. C. & J. Greenalls makes this triple-distilled, triple-filtered English vodka from wheat and spring water.

255. This premium whiskey is acknowledged to be the first of the small batch bourbons.

256. Produced in limited quantity, this 100% agave añejo was issued to commemorate Herradura's 125th anniversary.

257. What is the only variety of agave that tequila can legally be produced from?

258. According to Mexican law, how many times must tequila be distilled?

259. What is a reposado tequila?

260. What is an añejo tequila?

261. What is Agavero?

262. What is Goldschläger?

263. What is the difference between white and gold rum?

264. Who is credited with creating the first silver (blanco) rum?

265. This is the oldest distillery on the island of Jamaica.

266. This small batch, hand blended Trinidadian rum is aged a minimum of 12 years in charred American oak barrels.

267. This Bacardi rum is made in Puerto Rico, aged for one year in oak barrels and then filtered to remove its color.

268. This famous rum was created in 1910 and its name commemorates the total solar eclipse that occurred that year.

269. This distiller was granted to the first license to commercially produce tequila in 1795.

270. This chateau was honored as the "Purveyor by Special Appointment to the Court of Napoléon III."

271. This cognac is comprised of brandies from the finest vintages, some exceeding 200 years in age with the youngest brandy being from 1930.

272. Created in 1860, this rum is considered the national spirit of Bermuda.

273. Founded in 1870, this estate-produced tequila only makes 100% agave tequilas.

274. This super-premium French vodka is distilled in small batches from a choice blend of grains and limestone-filtered water from the Genté Springs in Champagne.

275. This French, aquamarine liqueur is made from triple-distilled vodka, aged cognac and a proprietary blend of natural tropical fruit juice.

276. Created in 1863 in Turin, Italy, it is the leading exported brand of vermouth.

277. Introduced in 1998, this brand of rum is blended on Anguilla and is comprised of nine pot-distilled, French oak aged rums.

L'Esprit de COURVOISIER

278. This 100% agave tequila from Sauza is triple-distilled and bottled unaged within 24 hours of distillation.

279. Introduced in 1932, this brand of vodka is made outside of Helsinki from six-row barley and glacier-fed spring water.

SECTION 2

PROFESSIONAL MIXOLOGY

The Who, What, Where, When and Why of Bartending

What was the
first London Dry Gin? The
majority of the world's vodkas
are distilled from what product? Where was
the Bacardi Rum distillery located before it moved to
Puerto Rico? What is the primary flavor of famed Disaronno Originale Amaretto? Where is Seagram's 7 Crown Blended Whiskey produced?
How does the pear get into the bottle of Poire William Eau-de-vie? What brand is
acknowledged as the first 100% blue agave tequila imported into the U.S.? How do
almond-flavored liqueurs derive their flavor? What liqueur was formulated by 16th
century alchemists in Europe as a medicinal elixir? What ingredient in sambuca, ouzo
and Pernod turns these liqueurs cloudy when poured over ice or mixed with water?
What whisky was introduced in 1939 to commemorate the unprecedented visit of
King George and Queen Elizabeth to Canada? What is the primary botanical in
nearly all brands of gin? With regards to the distilling of gin, what are botanicals?
What is the technical difference between lagers and ales? What is the principle
character difference between lagers and ales? What liqueur is actually a bottled gin
sling cocktail, a drink originated at a London restaurant in the late 1800s? What is the
best-selling brand of Goldwasser? The recipe for what renowned liqueur was
purportedly brought to Scotland by Bonnie Prince Charlie in 1745? What famous Scotch
whisky-based liqueur is made on the Isle of Skye? What famous American whiskey was
the first to be marketed in a square-shaped bottle? Which is aged longer, Wild Turkey
Black Label or White Label Bourbon? What famous Russian vodka is infused with lemon
essence? What product is most closely associated with solera aging? What country
does sherry originally come from? Baileys Original Irish Cream is made from chocolate,
coffee, cream and what distilled spirit? What liqueur bears the initials D.O.M. on its label?
Chambord Royale Liqueur has the rich flavor of what fruit? Other than color,
what is the principle difference between Blue
Curaçao and Triple

280. What is another name for quinine water?

281. What liquor is the spirituous base for the classic cocktail, the Caipirissma?

282. What two major categories of whiskies are written without an "e" in the word whisk(e)y?

283. How did the term, "bruised Martini," originate?

284. How do you convert a Cosmopolitan into a White Cosmopolitan?

285. What is the difference between a Kir and a Kir Royale?

286. How many liters is a magnum?

287. The combination of Angostura bitters and club soda is the long accepted bar remedy for what ailment?

288. In what order are the three ingredients poured into a B-52?

289. What is a frappé?

290. What is the purpose behind heating a snifter before serving a brandy neat?

291. What does the mixology instruction "over and up" mean?

292. What is a "bourbon and branch?"

293. What is "seasoned" ice?

294. Which vermouth is used to make a Southern Comfort Manhattan?

295. What is the continental term for a liquor served on the rocks?

296. The original Manhattan recipe called for Italian vermouth, bourbon or rye whiskey, and what other ingredient?

297. How did the term "proof" originate as the measure of alcohol potency?

298. What is the difference between a liqueur and a cordial?

299. What does the term "straight up" mean?

300. What is the more commonly used name for a double old fashion glass?

301. What is the difference between a Madras and a Seabreeze?

302. What drink originated in colonial India and obtained its name from a carpenter's tool of that era?

303. What carbonated mixer is used to prepare a buck, chiller and highball?

304. What two mixers are used to prepare a Presbyterian?

305. How is a "sweet" Manhattan prepared?

306. How is a drink to be prepared if the recipe calls for it to be "built?"

307. What does the mixology term "neat" mean?

308. What is the metric equivalent to the "fifth?"

309. What solution is used in the third sink compartment behind the bar?

310. When making a "Scotch rocks with a splash," what does "splash" refer to?

311. The Bocci Ball is prepared with what famous liqueur?

312. What is the name given to the combination of Gosling's Rum and ginger beer?

313. What does the mixology term "float" mean?

314. What is a mist?

315. How many ounces in a liter?

316. What is the name for a vodka gimlet made with triple sec added?

317. What name is given to a Martini garnished with a cocktail onion?

318. What drink requires the use of a "bar muddler" in its preparation?

319. What will club soda poured into an empty glass reveal about the glass?

320. What popular drink is named for a Californian surfer?

321. American soldiers fighting in Cuba during the Spanish-American War popularized what now-famous drink?

322. What name is given to the combination of champagne and orange juice?

323. What is the visible indicator that citrus juice has spoiled?

324. What two fortified wines are used most frequently behind a commercial bar?

325. What is added to a glass of beer to change it into a "Red Beer?"

326. In the movies, what drink did James Bond immortalize?

327. If a distilled spirit is 90 proof, how much alcohol by volume does it contain?

328. What is the garnish for sambuca served neat?

329. This glass is considered preferable to the snifter for appreciating brandy neat.

330. What type of bitters is used to make the New Orleans classic cocktail, the Sazerac?

331. What poultry product is used to make a Ramos Fizz?

332. How many ounces in a pony glass?

333. Which side of the lemon twist faces the glass before twisting?

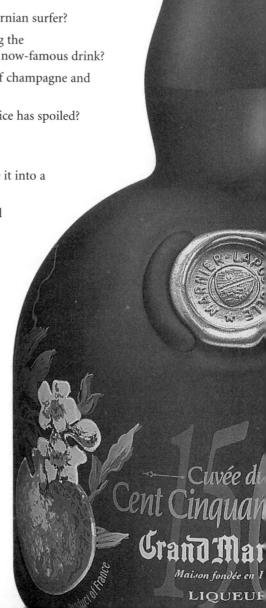

HOW'S YOUR LINKAGE WITH THE PAST?

This trivia challenge concerns itself with the genealogy of some of the most famous concoctions of the modern era.

1. This effervescent, fruit-laced concoction was first devised at Harry's Bar in Venice, Italy during World War II.

2. Created by Fernand Petiot at Harry's New York Bar in Paris in 1924, this famous drink was named after the unfortunate daughter of King Henry VIII.

3. This hot, Kahlúa-based specialty was created by George Bullington at Bully's Restaurant in southern California and dubbed the "George Coffee" in Hawaiian.

4. This drink originated in France during World War I and was named after a famed 75mm artillery piece.

5. This classic cocktail originated in San Francisco in the mid-1880's as the "Martinez Cocktail."

6. What classic tropical drink was invented by Vic Bergeron (Trader Vic) and was originally garnished with a fresh orchid?

7. This classic mixed drink originated at the Louisville Pendernis Club and was first served to famed bourbon producer, Colonel James Pepper.

8. The Buena Vista Cafe located at Fisherman's Wharf in San Francisco is credited with popularizing what famous hot drink?

9. This colorful tropical concoction actually originated at the Zanzibar Club in London.

10. The combination of Pernod and Champagne was popularized and named in honor of what great American author?

11. This famous tall drink was created by a London waiter at the turn of the century and obtained its name from the sweetened gin used in its preparation?

12. What drink recipe was invented by Don the Beachcomber and advertised "only one to a customer?"

13. What classic cocktail was created in honor of Jenny Jerome, the mother of Sir Winston Churchill, for her visit to a famous New York club in the mid-1870s?

14. What is the name given to the original "knock-out" drink, a concoction that was probably laced with chloral hydrate?

15. Which wine-based drink is named after a mayor of Dijon, France?

16. This famous rum based drink originated in 1954 at the Caribe Hilton Hotel, the name of which means, "strained pineapple."

17. What legendary mixologist invented the Blue Blazer?

18. What traditional hangover cure is named after a cowboy who in a fevered delirium cried out to his friends to bring him "his oyster?"

19. What classic rum drink was named for a mine located near Santiago, Cuba at the turn of the century?

20. What drink is closely associated with the running of the Kentucky Derby?

Answers on page 107.

334. How is Bloody Mary mix converted into Bloody Bull mix?

335. What carbonated mixer is used to make a "rickey?"

336. What piece of bar equipment is used to make a Pousse Café?

337. What is a cappuccino?

338. What is seltzer water?

339. What is simple syrup?

340. What is the name given to a Long Island Iced Tea made with an added splash of cranberry juice?

341. What is the difference between a Sombrero and a Smith & Kerns?

342. What bitters is used to make a Champagne Cocktail?

343. What is the standard serving portion for an aperitif wine?

344. What is the name given to the combination of vodka, cranberry and pineapple juice?

345. What drink is credited with introducing vodka into the mainstream of American drinking?

346. The introduction of this liqueur gave rise to the mega-popular Appletini.

347. What is a short shaker?

348. What is a topless margarita?

349. What is the name given to a red beer with an egg yolk floating on the surface?

350. Where is the speed rack located?

351. What is a Parfait?

352. What is bar time?

353. What are congeners?

354. The term "dog house" is jargon for what part of the bar?

355. With respect to mixology, what unit of measurement is a dash?

356. What is a flash blend?

357. What is ginger beer?

358. What is a horse's neck?

359. With respect to mixology, what is a punt or kick-up?

360. What is an overflow pipe?

361. What would it mean if one's drawer was short?

362. What is a Black Velvet?

BRUSHING UP ON YOUR PROFESSIONAL JARGON (PART I)

Benjamin Franklin once said that misusing a word was like ringing the bell of ignorance. While experience is the best way to become familiar with the lexicon of our business, it is fortunately not the only way. To that end, here's part one of our quiz on bar and beverage jargon.

1. Back	A. A party of two guests
2. Breakage	B. The liquor bottles emptied during the course of a shift
3. Comp Sheet	C. A term synonymous with club soda
4. Count	D. A ribbed rubber object used under glassware when making drinks
5. Doghouse	
6. Deuce	E. The primary work area for a bartender
7. Fifth	F. A narrow ledge that runs the length of the bar top
8. Muddle	G. The total number of reservations booked for lunch or dinner
9. On & Over	
10. Pour Mat	H. A device used to hold bottles positioned in front of a bartender
11. Rail	I. Jargon for the liquor display case
12. Seltzer	J. A liquor bottle containing 1/5th of a gallon (25.6 oz.)
13. Speed Rack	K. An iced glass of water that accompanies a cocktail
14. Three Top	L. Preparing a cocktail in a mixing glass, then straining it over ice
15. Well/Station	
	M. A table set with three place settings
	N. To crush the fruit contents in a glass
	O. A form used to record and track drinks given away

1.-K 2.-B 3.-O 4.-G 5.-I 6.-A 7.-J 8.-N 9.-L 10.-D 11.-F 12.-C 13.-H 14.-M 15.-E

363. What is a bar die?

364. What is a bar par?

365. What is the difference between a mist and frappé?

366. What classic rum drink was named for a mine located near Santiago, Cuba at the turn of the century?

367. What is a Black Velveteen?

368. What rum drink recipe was invented by Don the Beachcomber and advertised "only one to a customer?"

369. This bottled juice has been made in St. Albans, England, since the late 1700's from the reconstituted juice of West Indian limes.

370. What is orgeat syrup?

371. What is "pink gin?"

372. What is a liquor gun?

373. What is flaked ice?

374. What liqueur is floated on top of a tall Screwdriver to turn it into a Harvey Wallbanger?

375. What is grenadine syrup flavored with?

376. This French, non-alcoholic water is perfumed with the scent of orange blossoms and is invaluable in preparing a Ramos Fizz.

377. When someone orders a Dubonnet, is the Blanc or Rouge version being requested?

378. What is the difference between a Wine Spritzer and a Wine Cooler?

379. What is the difference between a Chi-Chi and a Piña Colada?

380. What is the origin of the phrase "86 someone?"

381. When is the combination of gin and dry vermouth not called a Martini?

382. This classic cocktail was introduced at a swank function honoring, among others, Lady Jenny Jerome, the mother of Sir Winston Churchill, in New York in the mid-1870s?

BRUSHING UP ON YOUR PROFESSIONAL JARGON (PART II)

Benjamin Franklin once said that misusing a word was like ringing the bell of ignorance. While experience is the best way to become familiar with the lexicon of our business, it is fortunately not the only way. To that end, here's part two of our quiz on bar and beverage jargon.

1. Bar Die

2. Build

3. Corkage

4. Cover

5. Draw

6. Flash Blend

7. Jigger

8. Mist

9. Over Proof

10. Quinine

11. Reach-in

12. Simple Syrup

13. Spritzer

14. Up Mixer

15. With

A. A fee charged to a guest who brings a bottle of wine into a restaurant

B. An under-the-counter refrigerator situated behind the bar

C. An iced drink made with wine and club soda

D. A solution made with equal parts of water and sugar

E. A request for a mug to be served with a bottle of beer

F. A mixer synonymous with tonic water

G. An electronic device resembling a milkshake mixer

H. Technical name for the bar's front structure

I. A liquor served over crushed ice

J. A restaurant table place setting (also refers to an entrance fee)

K. Preparing a drink directly into its service glass

L. A method of rapidly preparing a drink in a blender

M. A liquid measure equaling 1.5 ounces

N. A spirit containing over 57.1% alcohol by volume

O. To pour a draft beer

1.-H 2.-K 3.-A 4.-J 5.-O 6.-L 7.-M 8.-I 9.-N 10.-F 11.-B 12.-D 13.-C 14.-G 15.-E

383. The combination of Godiva, Kahlúa, Disaronno Amaretto and ice cream has the same flavor and name of what popular Italian dessert?

384. This famous drink must legally be prepared with Bacardi Light Rum?

385. This mainstream drink received its name after its inventor stirred it with a tool from his tool box.

386. What is the name given to the original "knock-out" drink, a concoction that was probably laced with chloral hydrate?

387. What name is given to the layered combination of brown crème de cacao and cream?

388. What are the two primary components of Collins mixer?

389. What is a shandy gaff?

390. How does the method of affixing sugar to the rim of a glass differ from that used for salt?

391. How is a short highball prepared?

392. What does the term "breakage" mean?

393. What is a "corkage fee?"

394. What is a "two-top?"

395. What is a French 75?

396. What is the difference between a French 75 and a French 125?

397. Why is vermouth always used before the liquor when making a Martini or Manhattan?

398. What is the standard garnish on a whiskey sour?

399. What name is given to a Vodka Collins made with gin instead of vodka?

400. What rum is marketed as the "Planter's Punch brand?"

401. What is the purpose behind heating a coffee glass prior to serving a hot drink?

402. What is gomme syrup?

403. What is a Black and Tan?

404. What is a tall highball?

405. What is a Caipirinha?

406. What does the designation "V.S.O.P." on a Cognac label stand for?

407. What two ingredients combine with Campari to make a Negroni?

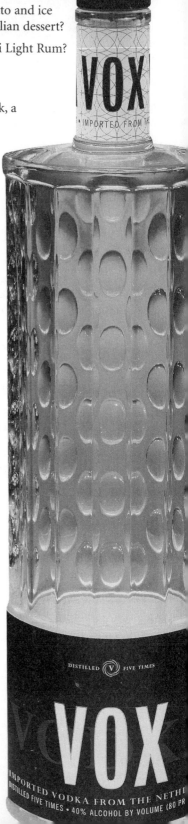

GREAT BARTENDERS DO IT ON THE ROCKS

The popularity of rock drinks has endured primarily because of their inherent simplicity. Long a mainstay of American mixology, they are able to deliver the goods unfettered by extraneous ingredients. Rock drinks feature a base liquor and are modified by a liqueur or two.

Being well versed in the world of rock drinks is essential for any aspiring bartender. Here then is a little harmless quiz to check out your familiarity with this noble drink category. Please note that many of these drinks are also served straight up or neat in a snifter.

1. Amber Cloud
2. Brave Bull
3. Cosmopolitan
4. Dirty Mother
5. Frappé
6. French Connection
7. Full Moon
8. Godfather
9. Godmother
10. Gold Rush
11. Kamikaze
12. Mist
13. Mudslide
14. Russian Quaalude
15. Rusty Nail
16. Sicilian Kiss
17. Silk Panties
18. Silver Bullet
19. Smith & Kerns
20. Smith & Wesson
21. Snow Shoe
22. Sombrero
23. Vodka Gimlet
24. White Bull
25. White Spider

A. Kahlúa + cream
B. Equal parts of Grand Marnier & Disaronno Amaretto
C. Scotch + Disaronno Amaretto
D. Bourbon + Peppermint Schnapps
E. Requested liquor poured over crushed ice
F. Kahlúa + cream + cola
G. Vodka + Disaronno Amaretto
H. Gold Tequila + Grand Marnier + lime juice
I. Vodka + Triple Sec + lime juice
J. Scotch + Drambuie
K. Stolichnaya Vodka + Frangelico + Kahlúa + Baileys
L. Vodka + Kahlúa + Baileys Irish Cream
M. Vodka + Peach Schnapps
N. Requested liqueur poured over crushed ice
O. Brandy + Kahlúa + cream
P. Tequila + White Crème de Menthe
Q. Equal parts of Disaronno Amaretto & Southern Comfort
R. Equal parts of VS Cognac & Grand Marnier
S. Kahlúa + cream + club soda
T. Tequila + Kahlúa
U. Citrus Vodka + Cointreau + lime juice + cranberry juice
V. Vodka + lime juice
W. Tequila + Kahlúa + cream
X. Vodka + White Crème de Menthe
Y. VS Cognac + Galliano

1.-Y 2.-T 3.-U 4.-O 5.-N 6.-R 7.-B 8.-C 9.-G 10.-H 11.-I 12.-E 13.-L 14.-K 15.-J 16.-Q 17.-M 18.-P 19.-S 20.-F 21.-D 22.-A 23.-V 24.-W 25.-X

408. How is a Mudslide prepared?

409. What is a Mojito?

410. What is the name of the cocktail that is similar to a Margarita, but made with brandy instead of tequila?

WHAT'S YOUR ALCOHOL IQ?

What
First London
majority of the
are distilled from what
the Bacardi Rum distillery
Puerto Rico? What is the primary
male Amaretto? Where is Seagram's 7
How does the pear get into the bottle of
acknowledged as the first 100% blue agave
almond-flavored liqueurs derive their flavor?
century alchemists in Europe as a medicinal
and Pernod turns these liqueurs cloudy
What whisky was introduced in 1939 to
King George and Queen Elizabeth to
nearly all brands of gin? With regards to
What is the technical difference between
character difference between lagers and
sling cocktail, a drink originated at a London
best-selling brand of Goldwasser? The
purportedly brought to Scotland by Bonnie
whisky-based liqueur is made on the Isle of
the first to be marketed in a square-shaped
Black Label or White Label Bourbon? What
essence? What product is most closely
does sherry originally come from? Baileys
coffee, cream and what distilled spirit? What
Chambord Royale Liqueur has the rich
what is the principle
Curaçao

was the
Dry Gin? The
world's vodkas
product? Where was
located before it moved to
flavor of famed Disaronno Origi-
Crown Blended Whiskey produced?
Poire William Eau-de-vie? What brand is
tequila imported into the U.S.? How do
What liqueur was formulated by 16th
elixir? What ingredient in sambuca, ouzo
when poured over ice or mixed with water?
commemorate the unprecedented visit of
Canada? What is the primary botanical in
the distilling of gin, what are botanicals?
lagers and ales? What is the principle
ales? What liqueur is actually a bottled gin
restaurant in the late 1800s? What is the
recipe for what renowned liqueur was
Prince Charlie in 1745? What famous Scotch
Skye? What famous American whiskey was
bottle? Which is aged longer, Wild Turkey
famous Russian vodka is infused with lemon
associated with solera aging? What country
Original Irish Cream is made from chocolate,
liqueur bears the initials D.O.M. on its label?
flavor of what fruit? Other than color,
difference between Blue
and Triple

411. A frozen Margarita has the same alcohol potency as a margarita served on the rocks. True/False

412. There is approximately the same amount of ethyl alcohol in a normal serving of 86.8 proof whiskey, draft or bottled beer, and white table wine. True/False

413. The alcohol present in liquor, beer and wine has the same impact on a person's blood alcohol concentration (BAC). True/False

414. When a person drinks distilled spirits, his or her BAC will rise faster and higher than were the person to have consumed an equivalent amount of either beer or wine. True/False

415. A person can become just as intoxicated drinking beer or wine as when drinking distilled spirits. True/False

416. A Manhattan served on the rocks is less alcoholically potent than a Manhattan served straight-up. True/False

417. The more alcohol that is absorbed into the bloodstream, the more impaired a person will become. True/False

418. The rate alcohol is absorbed into the bloodstream has only a minor affect on alcohol-induced impairment. True/False

419. Approximately 80% of the alcohol consumed enters the bloodstream directly through the lining of the stomach walls. True/False

420. A small percentage of alcohol passes through the small intestine unabsorbed in food matter and is eliminated. True/False

421. The presence of food in the stomach will slow the absorption rate of alcohol into the bloodstream. True/False

422. The pyloric valve plays a large role in determining how rapidly alcohol passes through the stomach and into the small intestine. True/False

423. The more food present in the stomach, the more the absorption rate of alcohol is delayed. True/False

424. The rise in BAC is more rapid when a person drinks alcohol with a meal. True/False

425. Fatty foods tend to cause the absorption rate of alcohol to increase. True/False

426. Foods that are high in carbohydrates absorb alcohol in the stomach, causing the absorption rate to decrease. True/False

427. The use of drugs or medicines does not increase the absorption rate of alcohol. True/False

428. Impairment often increases when alcohol and drugs are consumed simultaneously. True/False

429. Carbonation in a beverage tends to slow the absorption of alcohol into the bloodstream. True/False

430. Emotional stress, worry or anxiety may initially cause absorption rate to decrease. True/False

431. A person's disposition or mood can alter normal absorption and cause the alcohol to be "dumped" into the small intestine. True/False

432. Over 20% of the alcohol in the blood is absorbed by fatty tissue. True/False

433. The brain, muscles and central nervous system achieve relatively low concentrations of alcohol. True/False

434. The more a person weighs, the less BAC rises per ounce of alcohol consumed. True/False

435. In a man of average build, BAC will predictably rise 0.02% per ounce of spirits consumed. True/False

436. Body fat content has a direct impact on the rate of intoxication. True/False

437. A woman's BAC rises at the same rate as a man's per ounce of alcohol consumed. True/False

438. Since alcohol is absorbed at a constant rate, the pace that someone drinks alcohol will not affect BAC. True/False

439. The proof of a spirit will not appreciably affect BAC. True/False

440. Conventional wisdom states that anyone at a BAC of 0.1% will exhibit signs of impairment. True/False

441. A tall rum & cola is more potent than a regularly prepared rum & cola. True/False

442. The type of alcoholic beverage will not affect a person's rate of intoxication. True/False

443. Ethyl alcohol is toxic to the human physiology. True/False

444. A small percentage of the blood alcohol is detoxified through evaporation in the lungs. True/False

445. Alcohol is detoxified primarily through the function of the liver. True/False

446. The human physiology detoxifies alcohol at a fixed rate of approximately one ounce every two hours. True/False

447. BAC decreases at a rate of 0.015% per hour. True/False

448. The rate a person consumes alcohol directly affects the rate that it is detoxified from the blood. True/False

449. Light liquors are detoxified at a faster rate than dark liquors. True/False

450. If a person's BAC peaked at 0.2%, six hours later his or her probable BAC would still be over 0.1%. True/False

451. There is nothing within reason that can increase the rate a person detoxifies and sobers up. True/False

452. Despite being classified as a depressant, alcohol initially acts as a stimulant on the central nervous system. True/False

453. Exhilaration, loss of inhibition and a sense of calm or well being are accepted indications of a high BAC. True/False

454. As BAC rises, alcohol acts progressively more as a depressant. True/False

455. The majority of people begin exhibiting signs of impairment at a BAC of between 0.1% to .15%. True/False

456. After a person stops drinking, impairment will continue about 25% over the next hour. True/False

457. BAC usually peaks 60 minutes after a person stops drinking. True/False

458. As a person's BAC increases, sensible action and rational thinking steadily diminishes. True/False

459. Speaking increasingly louder is generally accepted as visible indicators of alcohol-induced intoxication. True/False

460. Loss of dexterity is generally accepted as visible indicators of alcohol-induced intoxication. True/False

461. Increased rate of consumption is generally accepted as visible indicators of alcohol-induced intoxication. True/False

462. Dilated pupils is generally accepted as visible indicators of alcohol-induced intoxication. True/False

463. Difficulty handling and lighting cigarettes is generally accepted as visible indicators of alcohol-induced intoxication. True/False

464. Aggressive and belligerent behavior is generally accepted as visible indicators of alcohol-induced intoxication. True/False

465. Anxious, nervous behavior is generally accepted as visible indicators of alcohol-induced intoxication. True/False

466. Loss of balance, unsteady gait is generally accepted as visible indicators of alcohol-induced intoxication. True/False

467. Excessive perspiration is generally accepted as visible indicators of alcohol-induced intoxication. True/False

468. Excessive tipping is generally accepted as visible indicators of alcohol-induced intoxication. True/False

469. Loss of visual acuity and eye contact is generally accepted as visible indicators of alcohol-induced intoxication. True/False

470. Loss of consciousness is generally accepted as visible indicators of alcohol-induced intoxication. True/False

471. Heightened appetite/insatiable hunger is generally accepted as visible indicators of alcohol-induced intoxication. True/False

472. Slurred speech or exaggerated, deliberate speech is generally accepted as visible indicators of alcohol-induced intoxication. True/False

473. Increased respiration rate is generally accepted as visible indicators of alcohol-induced intoxication. True/False

474. Rarely is the manager-on-duty in a better position to assess a person's level of intoxication than the individual serving the alcohol. True/False

475. If a patron orders a drink for someone not yet present, the bartender should prepare both drinks only if both of them have been paid for. True/False

476. Conventionally, management reserves the right to overrule a bartender's decision to refuse further service of alcohol to a patron. True/False

477. Bartenders shouldn't refuse further service of alcohol until a person begins exhibiting definite signs of intoxication. True/False

478. When in doubt as to the sobriety of a patron, the bartender should consult first with the manager-on-duty before serving the person alcohol. True/False

QUESTIONS FOR SEASONED PROS

What was the
first London Dry Gin? The
majority of the world's vodkas
are distilled from what product? Where was
the Bacardi Rum distillery located before it moved to
Puerto Rico? What is the primary flavor of famed Disaronno Originale Amaretto? Where is Seagram's 7 Crown Blended Whiskey produced?
How does the pear get into the bottle of Poire William Eau-de-vie? What brand is
acknowledged as the first 100% blue agave tequila imported into the U.S.? How do
almond-flavored liqueurs derive their flavor? What liqueur was formulated by 16th
century alchemists in Europe as a medicinal elixir? What ingredient in sambuca, ouzo
and Pernod turns these liqueurs cloudy when poured over ice or mixed with water?
What whisky was introduced in 1939 to commemorate the unprecedented visit of
King George and Queen Elizabeth to Canada? What is the primary botanical in
nearly all brands of gin? With regards to the distilling of gin, what are botanicals?
What is the technical difference between lagers and ales? What is the principle
character difference between lagers and ales? What liqueur is actually a bottled gin
sling cocktail, a drink originated at a London restaurant in the late 1800s? What is the
best-selling brand of Goldwasser? The recipe for what renowned liqueur was
purportedly brought to Scotland by Bonnie Prince Charlie in 1745? What famous Scotch
whisky-based liqueur is made on the Isle of Skye? What famous American whiskey was
the first to be marketed in a square-shaped bottle? Which is aged longer, Wild Turkey
Black Label or White Label Bourbon? What famous Russian vodka is infused with lemon
essence? What product is most closely associated with solera aging? What country
does sherry originally come from? Baileys Original Irish Cream is made from chocolate,
coffee, cream and what distilled spirit? What liqueur bears the initials D.O.M. on its label?
Chambord Royale Liqueur has the rich flavor of what fruit? Other than color,
what is the principle difference between Blue
Curaçao and Triple

WHAT YOU MIGHT NOT KNOW
ABOUT BEER

Evidence exists that proves man knew how to brew a fairly sophisticated beer 3800 years ago in Mesopotamia, well before the invention of the Barco-lounger. In fact, many of the same brewing techniques mastered by the Sumerians of the Bronze Age are still being used today by many of this country's brew masters.

Ancient Egyptians apparently also developed a fondness for beer. Recent discoveries have unearthed information indicating the slaves who built the pyramids near the present day Giza Plateau had five types of beer from which to choose and were given beer rations three times a day.

Today, beer remains one of the world's most widely produced, if not the most widely consumed, alcoholic potables. While a relatively simple substance — the basic components of most are barley, hops, yeast and water — the following questions on beer may not prove simple.

1. Originally brewed in Czechoslovakia, it is a
   bottom-fermented beer, typically golden-colored,
   dry and crisp; it is the most widely imitated style of beer.

2. This term is used to describe the relationship between the flavors of malt and hops in a beer.

3. This amber, hoppy brew is a hybrid made from both top- and bottom-fermenting yeasts; it is made only in San Francisco?

4. What does "Degrees Balling" measure?

5. Brewed with bottom-fermenting yeasts, it is the most widely produced type of beer in America?

6. Brewed in from roasted, unmalted barley, this beer has a bitter-hoppy taste, is full-bodied and extremely dark colored.

7. Made with top-fermenting yeasts, this type of brew is typically heavy-bodied, copper-colored (or darker), high in alcohol and most closely associated with English-style beers.

8. What is Krausening?

9. This term refers to the aroma and bouquet of a beer.

10. This type of Belgian, spontaneously fermented wheat beer is dry, full-bodied and usually aged in wooden casks.

11. Dry beers originated in this country.

12. This beer is a potent, full-bodied, bottom-fermented brew that originated in Einbeck, Germany.

13. Produced in both a sweet and dry, bitter version (Irish), this style of beer is typically full-bodied, extremely dark in color and brewed using roasted, unmalted barley.

14. The name given to American lagers with an alcohol content of 5% to 7.5% by volume.

15. This dark Bavarian lager is typically low in alcohol and brewed specifically for a German annual event.

16. This type of English draught is malty, moderately sweet, ranges in color from amber to dark brown and is brewed with top-fermenting yeasts.

17. Extremely popular in England, this draught is dry, full-bodied, amber to copper colored and lightly carbonated; when bottled, this beer is labeled as Pale Ale.

18. Brewed exclusively at monasteries in Belgium and the Netherlands, these beers are fruity, bottle-conditioned and made from top-fermenting yeasts.

19. This German wheat beer is dry, low in alcohol, has a slightly sharp taste and shares the same name with the city of its origin.

20. This style of brewing produces a dry, golden-blonde, bottom-fermented lager and is associated with this city in northern Germany.

21. This malty, dark-brown, bottom-fermented lager is associated with this city in Bavaria; it is produced in both a Helles and Dunkel version.

22. This Belgian wheat beer is dark red, the result of being flavored with cherries.

23. This amber, rich tasting French beer is brewed with top-fermenting yeasts; being cork-finished, it should be stored on its side like wine.

24. Fruity and copper-colored, this Belgian beer is brewed with top-fermenting yeasts, naturally conditioned in wooden casks and cork-finished.

25. This top-fermented, warm-conditioned white wheat beer is made only in Hoegaarden, Belgium.

Answers on page 108

479. Which results in a lower figure, measuring a beer's alcohol content by weight or by volume?

480. Brewed in Dusseldorf and Münster, this top-fermented beer is copper-colored and possesses a hoppy flavor.

481. This Martinique rhum is distilled from unfermented sugar cane juice and then aged and blended in Bordeaux, France.

482. What is Old Tom Gin?

483. This whiskey by Wild Turkey is a 110 proof, undiluted, unfiltered single cask bourbon.

484. This type of Belgian, spontaneously fermented wheat beer is dry, full-bodied and usually aged in wooden casks.

485. This yellow-hued, aromatic vodka is only produced in Eastern Poland and flavored with rare species of grass from which it derives its name.

486. What is a bottled-in-bond bourbon?

487. Brewed from roasted unmalted barley, this beer has a bitter-hoppy taste, is full-bodied and extremely dark colored.

488. This amber, rich-tasting French beer is brewed with top-fermenting yeasts; being cork-finished, it should be stored on its side like wine.

489. This distillery in Tullahoma, Tennessee has been producing sour mash whiskey since 1870.

490. This descriptive phrase is used to identify the small amount of whisky that is lost from a cask through evaporation.

491. This Belgian wheat beer is dark red in color, the result of being flavored with cherries.

492. What rum did Paul Revere quaff after his famous midnight ride?

493. This golden Norwegian Aquavit is aged in wooden casks stored in the holds of ships bound for the equator.

494. What is a "Belgium lace?"

495. What is Aguardiente?

In the old days before white zinfandel and light beer, the only educational requirements necessary to leave the bartending ranks for the glamour and social prestige of "bar manager" was to know the difference between gin and vodka and successfully avoid the attention of the GM.

Those requirements have changed just a bit. The marketplace has become decidedly more competitive. Bar managers today are far more savvy and knowledgeable than before. Just to prove our point, here's a little trivia challenge on modern bar mathematics. Sharpen your pencils, this quiz is nasty.

1. Divide the number of ounces in a magnum of California cabernet sauvignon by the percentage of alcohol in a bottle of Budweiser.

2. Multiply the number found on the label of Rolling Rock by the number of ounces in a keg of American beer.

3. Add the number of ounces in a gallon and the percentage of alcohol in a bottle of Red Label Absolut vodka, and then subtract the number of ounces in a split of champagne.

4. Multiply the number of crowns in Seagram's blended whiskey by the age Chivas Regal, then multiply the result by the number of ounces in a jigger.

5. Add the year that prohibition in the US was repealed to the number of ounces in a bottle of wine.

6. Multiply the alcoholic proof of Bailey's Irish Cream by the denomination on a "double sawbuck."

7. Multiply the number of ounces in a liter by the alcoholic proof of Wild Turkey White Label.

8. Add the respective ages of Glenlivet and Glenfiddich single malts, then multiply that sum by the percentage of agave used to make Patrón tequila.

9. Divide the age of Chivas Regal Royal Salute by the number of generations represented on a bottle of Sauza añejo tequila.

10. Subtract the number of ounces in a 750ml bottle of spirits from the alcoholic proof of Jack Daniel's, then multiply the remainder by he number contained in the phrase, "Jack Daniel's Old Number ___."

1. $50.7/4.8 = 10.56$; 2. $33 \times 1984 = 65,472$; 3. $128 + 50 - 6.35 = 171.65$; 4. $7 \times 12 \times 1.5 = 126$; 5. $1933 + 25.4 = 1958.4$; 6. $34 \times 20 = 680$; 7. $33.8 \times 101 = 3413.8$; 8. $12 + 12 \times 100 = 2400$; 9. $21/3 = 7$; 10. $98 - 25.4 \times 7 = 424.2$

WINE
VIN
VINO
VINHO
WEIN
QUIZ

For some the following questions may be easy pickin's, for others they may be the grapes of wrath. Nevertheless, uncorking a few questions regarding one of the oldest potables seems overdue. So dust off those thinking caps, swirl and spit.

1. This highly sought-after French red wine is bottled extremely young and cannot be legally sold before the third Thursday in November.

2. Stags Leap District is a renowned appellation within this famous California wine-growing county.

3. This burrowing plant louse devastated European vineyards between 1860 and 1880 and its descendants are now ravaging Californian grape vines.

4. Made entirely from Chardonnay, wine from this famous appellation in Côte d'Or, Burgundy is France's most expensive dry white wine.

5. This category of American wines is a blend of two or more varieties of grapes and is often labeled as a red or white table wine with a vintage and appellation.

6. Implemented in 1963, this system established standards for origin, grape variety, yield and quality for labeling Italian wines.

7. The identifying term for the smell of fresh fruit in young wines; not to be confused with "bouquet," which is characteristic of aged, more complex wines.

8. It is the grape variety of California's premier white wine, Burgundy's Pouilly-Fuisse and nearly all of Blanc de Blanc Champagne.

9. This is the palest, lightest and usually driest type of Sherry.

10. A small yet distinguished wine-producing village in Germany's Mosel Valley renowned for its white wine.

11. This French wine-producing appellation in Bordeaux is noted for its sweet golden wines, including the distinguished Château d'Yquem.

12. Located near San Francisco, this famous California wine-producing county encompasses such appellations as Russian River Valley, Alexander Valley and Dry Creek Valley.

13. This extremely sweet and expensive German wine is made in the Rhine and Mosel from hand-selected grapes left to wither on the vine late into the harvest.

14. This wine-producing region in north central Italy produces such famous wines as Chianti and Brunello di Montalchino.

15. Long used to soften Californian Cabernet Sauvignon, this grape variety has become a popular varietal wine on its own merits.

16. This system in France is used to control over 200 types of wines; identifying particular growing regions and establishes levels of quality within specific appellations.

17. Dubbed the "noble rot," it is a highly beneficial mold that results in grapes achieving a more concentrated flavor and sweetness.

18. A type of secondary fermentation caused by the introduction of lactobacillus bacteria that converts malic acid into lactic acid.

19. This type of Port is a blend of well-aged wines, pale in color with a distinctive amber edge and is relatively expensive.

20. This is a group of astringent, organic compounds derived from grape skins, stems and pips that dissolve into wine during fermentation and imbue it with depth, character and increased longevity.

1. Beaujolais Nouveau 2. Napa Valley 3. Phylloxera (Biotype B) 4. Le Montrachet 5. Meritage 6. Denominazione de Origine Controllata (DOC) 7. Aroma 8. Chardonnay 9. Fino 10. Piesport 11. Sauternes 12. Sonoma 13. Trockenbeerenauslese 14. Tuscany 15. Merlot 16. Appellation d'Origine Contrôlée (AOC) 17. Botrytis Cinerea 18. Malolactic fermentation 19. Tawny Port 20. Tannin

496. What is the generic name for French anise liqueurs such as Ricard and Pernod?

497. This mild caraway-flavored Kümmel is best known by what four initials?

498. Fruity and copper-colored, this Belgian beer is brewed with top-fermenting yeasts, naturally conditioned in wooden casks and cork-finished.

499. This Swiss chocolate liqueur has small squares of chocolate inside the bottle.

500. Aged 15 years, this label is the rarest of the Chartreuse liqueurs.

501. This popular European liqueur is made from wild purple plums.

502. The style of brewing associated with this city in northern Germany produces a dry, golden-blonde, bottom-fermented lager.

503. This malty, dark brown, bottom-fermented lager is associated with a city in Bavaria; it is produced in both a Helles and Dunkel version.

504. What is Fraise?

505. This famous New Orleans liqueur is made from pecans and vanilla.

506. The recipe for this Irish liqueur was lost until the late 1800s.

507. This top-fermented, warm-conditioned, white wheat beer is made only in Hoegaarden, Belgium.

508. What is the principle flavor of the French liqueur, Creme de Noisette?

509. This dark brown, bittersweet beer is called a wine to underscore its high alcohol content.

510. What is Himbeergeist?

511. This French liqueur is made by the Lapostelle family from passion fruit and Armagnac brandy.

512. This Austrian liqueur is made in Salzberg from semi-sweet chocolate and nougat.

513. This type of Kümmel is bottled warm, which causes sugar crystals to form on the bottom of the bottle.

514. This dark Bavarian lager is typically low in alcohol and brewed specifically for an annual celebration.

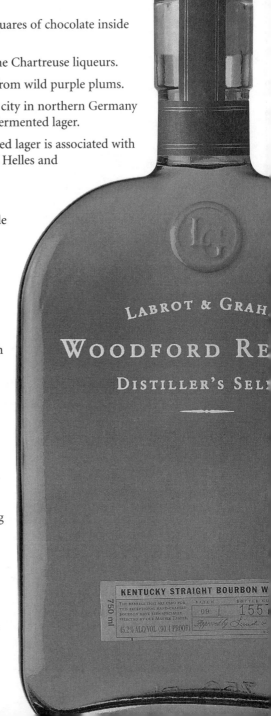

A single malt whisky is one in which all of the malt whiskies used in its blend are distilled at a single distillery. Unless stated to the contrary, single malts are carefully constructed from whiskies of different ages and wood finishes. Malt whiskies are typically aged in ex-bourbon barrels or sherry casks, although many distillers are now finishing their whiskies in ex-port pipes, French oak barrels or claret casks.

The significant factors in how good a malt is where the whisky is distilled, the quality of the water and where it is aged, which makes the location of the distillery of particular interest. For example, the climate in the southern part of Scotland is much different than it is in the north. Whiskies matured on the Scottish islands are greatly affected by the salty sea air.

So, what do you know about the single malts on your back bar? If a guest requests a brand that you don't stock, will you know malt to recommend in its place? To that end, we've created a little trivia challenge that will test your Single Malt Geography IQ.

For each brand of single malt whisky, identify it comes from Highlands (H), Lowlands (L), Islay (I), Campbeltown (C), Mull (M), Skye (S), or Orkney (O).

1. Aberlour

2. Auchentoshan

3. Balvenie

4. Bowmore

5. Dalmore

6. Dalwhinnie

7. Glenfarclas

8. Glenfiddich

9. Glengoyne

10. Glenkinchie

11. Glenlivet

12. Glenmorangie

13. Glenrothes

14. Highland Park

15. Lagavulin

16. Laphroaig

17. Scapa

18. Springbank

19. Talisker

20. Tobermoray

1.-H 2.-L 3.-H 4.-I 5.-H 6.-H 7.-H 8.-H 9.-H 10.-L 11.-H 12.-H 13.-H 14.-O 15.-I 16.-I 17.-O 18.-C 19.-S 20.-M

515. Made by Moët & Chandon, this product is the first and to-date only sparkling liqueur.

516. This French liqueur is made from, among other things, a blend of old brandies, orange Curaçao and Creme de Cacao.

517. These potent German beers usually end in the suffix "-ator."

518. This violet-petal liqueur is named after the French actress, Yvette Gilbert.

519. Produced in the People's Republic of China from a 600 year old recipe, this liqueur is made from six varieties of ginger, ginseng, herbs, honey and brandy.

520. This Basque liqueur is made from Armagnac, and rare herbs and flowers that grow only in the French Pyrenees.

521. Brewed for Catherine the Great, this English stout was originally cask-conditioned to endure the long Baltic voyage to St. Petersburg.

522. What is the flavor of Goldwasser?

523. This English liqueur is made from honey, lemon, orange, vanilla and freshly brewed tea.

524. Brewed exclusively in monasteries in Belgium and the Netherlands, these beers are fruity, bottle-conditioned and made from top-fermenting yeasts.

525. This German wheat beer is dry, low in alcohol, has a slightly sharp taste and bears the same name as the city of its origin.

526. This clear, low-proof liqueur made in Barbados is flavored with lime, almond, ginger and spices.

527. What creamy thick liqueur is made from egg yolks, sugar and brandy?

528. This aromatic European liqueur is made from citrus oils, citron, brandy and violet petals.

529. Also known as Arrack, this pale golden liqueur is made from a base of Batavia Arak.

TESTING YOUR VODKA GEOGRAPHY IQ

Vodka is a commodity nearly synonymous with Russia. The spirit originated there in the 12th century and was called *zhiznennia voda*, meaning "water of life," testimony to the near reverence the distillate had in early civilization. Wodka was first produced in Poland over 500 years ago. Those who savor vodkas with body and flavor eventually visit the brands produced in Poland.

The art of distilling vodka and the fascination over creating an essentially pure spirit is not confined to the Russia and Poland. Renowned brands of vodka are now available in the U.S. from the United Kingdom, Scandinavia and numerous points throughout the New World.

Vodka sales in America confirm that it is this country's spirit of choice. So, what do you know about the brands on your shelf? To that end, we've created a little trivia challenge that will test your Vodka Geography IQ.

1. Bäalta	A. Austria
2. Below 42°	B. Belarus
3. Boru	C. Belgium
4. Charodei	D. Canada
5. Christiania	E. England
6. Grey Goose	F. Estonia
7. Luksusowa	G. France
8. Magadanskaya	H. Georgia
9. Mezzaluna	I. Germany
10. Monopolowa	J. Holland
11. Pearl	K. Ireland
12. Türi	L. Italy
13. Level	M. Japan
14. Suntory	N. Lithuania
15. Tarkhuna	O. New Zealand
16. Three Olives	P. Norway
17. Tito's Handmade	Q. Poland
18. Van Gogh	R. Siberia
19. Van Hoo	S. Sweden
20. Wodka Gorbatschow	T. Ukraine
21. Zhitomirskaya Jubilee	U. United States

1.-N 2.-O 3.-K 4.-B 5.-P 6.-G 7.-Q 8.-R 9.-L 10.-A 11.-D 12.-F 13.-S 14.-M 15.-H 16.-E 17.-U 18.-J 19.-C 20.-I 21.-T.

530. This type of English draught is malty, moderately sweet, ranges in color from amber to dark brown and is brewed with top-fermenting yeasts.

531. Extremely popular in England, this draught is dry, full-bodied, amber to copper colored and lightly carbonated; when bottled, this beer is labeled as Pale Ale.

532. The Stags Leap District is a renowned appellation within this famous California wine-growing county.

533. This burrowing plant louse devastated European vineyards between 1860 and 1880 and its descendants are now ravaging Californian grape vines.

534. Sheep Dip's and Pig's Nose are examples of what type of spirit?

535. Where in Scotland are single malts Laphroaig and Lagavulin produced?

536. This famous London Dry Gin is actually distilled at Finsbury, England, which at one time was a heath spa known for the purity of its water.

537. Made in what was Soviet Georgia, this vodka has a greenish hue and the flavor of Tarkhuna grass.

538. Now distilled in Pennsylvania, this 4 year old, straight rye whiskey was originally distilled in Cincinnati.

539. Glenkinchie and Rosebank are preeminent examples of single malt whiskies made in this region of Scotland.

540. What is the name used to describe very old cognacs that have been removed from their casks and placed in glass decanters for later use in blending?

541. Cragganmore and Knockando are among the single malt whiskies made in what region of the Scottish Highlands?

542. What rum is occasionally flavored with such things such as coconut shells, limes, roots and raisins?

543. Swing is this distillery's 20 year old blended Scotch whisky.

544. This Jamaican rum distillery produces such labels as the 7 year old "Three Daggers" and the 63% alcohol by volume "Over Proof."

545. This 12 year old, Single Highland Malt Scotch is aged exclusively in oak casks previously used to age sherry.

546. "Oude" and "Jonge" are styles of this type of gin.

547. What is Stolichnaya Okhotnichya?

548. This pure grain vodka is made with artesian water and filtered through red granite chips.

549. This German brandy is made from French grapes, twice distilled in pot stills and aged in oak for 8 years.

550. Laird's is the producer of this famous American brandy.

551. If you saw the designation XXO on a label, what type of spirit would you be looking at?

552. Janeiro is the leading brand name of this type of Brazilian spirit.

553. What is Marc?

554. Similar in character to vodka, this Asian spirit has been distilled since the 1500s from grain, molasses or sweet potatoes.

555. This South American cane spirit is likely the oldest distilled spirit in the world.

556. What is cachaça?

557. This Italian liqueur is made from egg yolks and Marsala wine.

558. This triple distilled vodka has been made in a copper pot still in Holland for over 300 years.

559. Kolsch is a pale golden ale brewed exclusively in what country?

560. This dry Spanish liqueur is flavored with star anise.

561. This 80 proof French liqueur is similar in character to Benedictine yet remains less renown than its 110 proof counterpart.

562. This brand of pastis has been made in Marseilles, France since the 1930s.

563. This semi-sweet herbal liqueur is made in England and is named after a famous literary family.

564. This distillery first began producing whiskey in Dublin in 1780 and is known for such labels as "Crested Ten" and "White Label."

565. What is Havana Club?

566. This 1975 vintage single malt Scotch is finished in casks that contained burgundy from the Côte de Nuits wine region.

567. Micro-distilled in Bend, OR, this 95 proof gin is flavored with local juniper and indigenous botanicals.

568. This premium line of rum is the last to be distilled in the continental United States.

569. This ultra-premium, small batch bourbon by Jim Beam is aged for 20 years and finished in port casks.

570. This world-class American alembic brandy is distilled primarily from pinot noir and aged in Limousin barrels.

571. This preeminent brandy is produced at the country's oldest licensed distillery from a blend of five varieties of apples and aged in oak for 12 years.

GREAT AMERICAN SPIRITS

While there are many great countries in the world, we're really partial to the United States of America. It's probably because we were born here and we pay a lot of taxes. Anyway, America can lay claim to more than its fair share of great spirits and liqueurs.

The United States is garnering critical acclaim these days for more than just bourbon. There are now a slew of world-class vodkas and rums made between our shores. If that's news to you, check out this little quiz and test your level of familiarity with what America has to offer.

1. Buffalo Trace
2. Cascade Mountain
3. Conch Republic
4. Crater Lake
5. Domaine Charbay
6. Gentleman Jack
7. Germain-Robin
8. Hamptons
9. Hangar One
10. Jefferson's Reserve
11. Junipero
12. Knob Creek
13. Kona Gold
14. Liquid Ice
15. McCarthy's
16. Old Portero
17. Rare Breed
18. Sam Houston
19. Shakers
20. Spudka
21. Teton Glacier
22. Tito's Handmade
23. Triple Eight
24. Virginia Gentleman
25. Woodford Reserve

A. Range of small batch, pot distilled grain vodkas made in Alameda, California

B. Handcrafted alembic brandies distilled from California grape varietals

C. Gin distilled in Minnesota using yellow corn and an array of botanicals

D. Limited-release bourbon bottled undiluted, unfiltered and at barrel-proof

E. Small batch vodka alembic distilled from local grain and the spring water

F. Tennessee whiskey double barreled and mellowed in sugar maple charcoal

G. Micro-distilled gin made with botanicals indigenous to the Northwest

H. Range of rums made in Florida and distilled in continuous and pot stills

I. Small batch bourbon aged 15 years in heavily charred oak barrels

J. Small batch, triple-distilled bourbon made at the Labrot & Graham Distillery

K. Handmade, micro-distilled vodka produced in Austin from high-grade corn

L. Alembic distilled single malt made from malted rye in San Francisco

M. Ultra-premium vodkas distilled in Minnesota from grain and spring water

N. Small batch bourbon aged 9 years in deeply charred white oak barrels

O. Vodka distilled from potatoes and glacier-fed spring water in Oregon

P. Small batch, alembic gin made in San Francisco at the Anchor Distillery

Q. Range of alembic distilled vodkas made entirely from Midwest grain

R. Extremely small batch bourbon aged 10 years in heavily charred oak barrels

S. Vodka made in Idaho triple-distilled from potatoes and Rocky Mountain water

T. Small batch, pot distilled whiskey made in Oregon from peat-malted barley

U. Limited release bourbon made from corn, select rye and malted barley

V. Micro-distilled vodka made from organic corn on Nantucket Island

W. Small batch, pot distilled straight bourbon whiskey made in Fredericksburg

X. Hawaiian liqueur made from 100% Kona coffee beans

Y. Quadruple-distilled vodka made in Idaho from a blend of organic grains

1.-U 2.-G 3.-H 4.-E 5.-Q 6.-F 7.-B 8.-C 9.-A 10.-I 11.-P 12.-N 13.-X 14.-Y 15.-T 16.-L 17.-D 18.-R 19.-M 20.-O 21.-S 22.-K 23.-V 24.-W 25.-J

572. This small batch Idaho vodka is triple-distilled from potatoes and pure, deep Rocky Mountain water.

573. This 90.4 proof whiskey is made in Texas and mellowed with mesquite chips.

574. This ultra-premium Polish vodka is crafted from a singular blend of potato, wheat and rye.

575. This vodka is made in Dublin and quadruple-distilled in small batches from grain and spring water, then filtered through 10 feet of Atlantic oak charcoal.

576. Produced in Barbados by R.L. Seale & Company, this superior barrel-aged rum is finished in Spanish oak Oloroso sherry casks.

577. This ultra-premium rum is made in the traditional British naval style and is a blend of five, molasses-based, pure pot still rums from Jamaica and Guyana.

578. Bottled at a potent 110 proof, this ultra-premium gin from the Scottish firm Cadenhead's gets its unusual color and taste from saffron.

579. Self-described as the "world's most peculiar gin," this spirit is made from an infusion of juniper, coriander, citrus, rose petals and cucumber.

580. This ultra-premium tequila is a blend of silver and añejo 100% agave tequilas that are further aged in casks previously used to mature de Fussigny Cognac.

581. The final phase of maturation for this cognac involves being sent in Limousin oak barrels around the world on a 3-month ocean voyage.

582. This liqueur was originally produced by the alchemists in Danzig, Poland and contains 22-carat gold flakes.

583. The oldest Irish whiskey on the market, this extraordinary spirit was distilled in 1951 and aged for 36 years.

584. This is a BATF classification for an American lager with an alcohol by volume content of 5% to 7.5% by volume.

585. This Canadian whisky recently released a small-batch, 8-year old whisky aged in white oak barrels and double-matured in sherry casks.

586. The dramatic appearance of this recently released vodka from London is derived through a Burmese herb called the black catechu.

587. This super-premium French gin is triple-distilled in small batches and formulated using 19 different botanicals.

588. This hand-made, small-batch bourbon by at the McLain & Kyne Distillery is aged for 15-years in new white, heavily charred oak barrels.

589. Made in Oregon, this single malt whiskey is distilled in a pot still from malted barley peat-dried in Scotland.

590. What might well be the most exclusive and highly sought-after bourbon, this whiskey was distilled at the now defunct Michter Distillery in Pennsylvania.

591. This single malt Scotch is made in the world's northernmost distillery.

592. The Guinness Book of Records lists this label of brandy as the world's most expensive cognac.

593. This triple-distilled Bushmill's Irish whiskey is a blend of malted barleys aged up to nine years in Oloroso sherry oak casks.

594. This blended whisky combines 100 distinctive single malt whiskies produced from distilleries in every appellation throughout Scotland.

595. This famous London Dry Gin is the only premium gin distillery remaining in London.

596. This classic American straight rye whiskey is now distilled by Jim Beam.

597. This Johnnie Walker blend contains fifteen different 18-year-old single malt whiskies.

598. This famed cognac producer has the largest reserve of old cognacs with 250,000 barrels aging at all times.

599. This pioneering whiskey was the first brand to bottle a single barrel bourbon.

600. This ultra-premium, vintage-dated blended Irish whiskey is made at the Midleton Distillery in Cork.

601. This distillery's 10-year old whisky is the best selling single malt in Scotland.

602. Made at the Liviz Distillery in St. Petersburg, this super-premium wheat vodka is named for the numerous medals it has won.

603. The only malt produced on the island of Skye, it is the backbone of Johnnie Walker Red Label blend.

604. What is rhum?

605. What is the name of Wild Turkey's single barrel bourbon?

606. What are Rhum Vieux?

607. What is the difference between Rhum Vieux and Rhum Trés Vieux?

608. What cinnamon schnapps is made in Switzerland and bottled with a little something extra.

609. What is the other name for crème de almond?

610. This semi-sweet orange liqueur has a notable appearance.

611. What tequila-based liqueur is made in Mexico and flavor with the Damiana plant?

612. This triple-distilled liqueur is made from bitter Curaçao oranges.

BAR EXAMS

Entry Level, Intermediate and Advanced

W h a t
irst London
majority of the
are distilled from what
he Bacardi Rum distillery
Puerto Rico? What is the primary
ale Amaretto? Where is Seagram's 7
How does the pear get into the bottle of
acknowledged as the first 100% blue agave
almond-flavored liqueurs derive their flavor?
century alchemists in Europe as a medicinal
and Pernod turns these liqueurs cloudy
What whisky was introduced in 1939 to
King George and Queen Elizabeth to
nearly all brands of gin? With regards to
What is the technical difference between
character difference between lagers and
ling cocktail, a drink originated at a London
best-selling brand of Goldwasser? The
purportedly brought to Scotland by Bonnie
whisky-based liqueur is made on the Isle of
he first to be marketed in a square-shaped
Black Label or White Label Bourbon? What
essence? What product is most closely
does sherry originally come from? Baileys
coffee, cream and what distilled spirit? What
Chambord Royale Liqueur has the rich
what is the principle
Curaçao

was the
Dry Gin? The
world's vodkas
product? Where was
located before it moved to
flavor of famed Disaronno Origi-
Crown Blended Whiskey produced?
Poire William Eau-de-vie? What brand is
tequila imported into the U.S.? How do
What liqueur was formulated by 16th
elixir? What ingredient in sambuca, ouzo
when poured over ice or mixed with water?
commemorate the unprecedented visit of
Canada? What is the primary botanical in
the distilling of gin, what are botanicals?
lagers and ales? What is the principle
ales? What liqueur is actually a bottled gin
restaurant in the late 1800s? What is the
recipe for what renowned liqueur was
Prince Charlie in 1745? What famous Scotch
Skye? What famous American whiskey was
bottle? Which is aged longer, Wild Turkey
famous Russian vodka is infused with lemon
associated with solera aging? What country
Original Irish Cream is made from chocolate,
liqueur bears the initials D.O.M. on its label?
flavor of what fruit? Other than color,
difference between Blue
and Triple

To **download a user friendly format** (8.5"x 11") of the following tests, go to the following web address: **http://www.barmedia.com/bonus/**

TEST ONE — ENTRY LEVEL BAR EXAM

1. The majority of the world's vodkas are distilled from what product?
2. What is the predominant flavor of gin?
3. What is the difference between lagers and ales?
4. Which is aged longer, Wild Turkey Black or White Label?
5. Baileys Irish Cream is made from chocolate, coffee, cream and what distilled spirit?
6. What liqueur bears the initials D.O.M. on its label?
7. Chambord Royale Liqueur has the rich flavor of what fruit?
8. Other than color, what is the principle difference between blue Curaçao and triple sec?
9. Brewed with bottom-fermenting yeasts, it is the most widely produced type of beer in America.
10. This renowned German liqueur is made from 56 herbs, roots, fruit and gentian.
11. What spirit can be distilled from potatoes, rice, beets, grapes or grain?
12. What liquor is compounded by redistilling neutral grain spirits with berries, roots, bark, seeds and plant parts?
13. What is rum distilled from?
14. What is brandy distilled from?
15. This Italian anise-flavored liqueur is actually made from wild elderbush berries.
16. What famous liqueur is made with cognac and triple oranges?
17. What is the alcohol-base of Drambuie?
18. The House of Burrough has produced this London Dry Gin since the early 1800s.
19. Are most Scotch whiskies blended or straight?
20. First distilled in the 1830s by Scottish immigrants, this type of whisky is made from a blend of rye, corn and barley.
21. What label of rum is marketed as the "Planter's Punch Brand?"
22. Which is darker, bourbon or Scotch?
23. What gives red wine the color lacking in white wine?
24. Which of the basic liquors is usually poured at the highest proof?
25. Is schnapps a liquor or liqueur?
26. Crown Royal is a super-premium label of what type of spirits?
27. What is Johnnie Walker Black Label?

28. What happens to tequila when it is aged in wood?

29. What is another name for quinine?

30. In what order are the three ingredients poured into a B-52?

31. Which vermouth is used to make a Southern Comfort Manhattan?

32. What does the term "straight up" mean?

33. What two mixers are used to prepare a "Presbyterian?"

34. How is a drink to be prepared and served if the recipe calls for it to be "built?"

35. Unless instructed otherwise, a "splash" always refers to what product?

36. What is the name for a Vodka Gimlet made with triple sec?

37. What name is given to a Martini garnished with cocktail onions?

38. What is simple syrup?

39. What two ingredients are used to make a Wine Spritzer?

40. What liqueur is floated on top of a tall Screwdriver to turn it into a Harvey Wallbanger?

41. What is the difference between a Wine Spritzer and a Wine Cooler?

42. What is the difference between a Chi-Chi and Piña Colada?

43. Why is vermouth always used before the liquor when making a Martini or Manhattan?

44. What name is given to a Vodka Collins made with gin instead of vodka?

45. What rum is used to make a Planter's Punch?

46. A frozen Margarita has the same alcohol potency as a Margarita served on the rocks. (True or False)

47. The alcohol present in liquor, beer and wine has the same impact on a person's blood alcohol concentration (BAC). (True or False)

48. A person can become just as intoxicated drinking beer or wine as when drinking distilled spirits. (True or False)

49. The more alcohol that is absorbed into the bloodstream, the more impaired a person will become. (True or False)

50. The presence of food in the stomach will retard the absorption rate of alcohol into the bloodstream. (True or False)

TEST ONE — ENTRY LEVEL ANSWER KEY

1. The majority of vodkas are distilled from corn.

2. Juniper

3. Lagers are brewed with bottom-fermenting yeasts while ales are brewed using top-fermenting yeasts.

4. Wild Turkey White Label Bourbon is aged for 8 years.

5. Irish whiskey

6. Benediction D.O.M.

7. Black raspberry

8. Triple sec is drier than Curaçao.

9. Lager

10. Jägermeister

11. Vodka

12. Gin

13. Rum is distilled from fresh sugar cane juice, molasses or fermented sugar cane syrup.

14. Brandy is distilled from the fermented mash of fruit.

15. Sambuca

16. Grand Marnier Cordon Rouge

17. Single Highland Malt Scotch whisky

18. Beefeater London Distilled Dry Gin

19. The majority of Scotch whiskies are blended

20. Canadian whisky

21. Myers's Original Dark Jamaican Rum

22. As a result of being aged in wooden casks, the insides of which have been charred, bourbons are typically darker than Scotch whiskies.

23. When making red wine, the skins are left in contact with the juice after the grapes have been pressed. Within the skins are pigments that give the grapes their color. These pigments, in turn, give color to the resulting wine.

24. London dry gins usually range in alcohol content between 90 and 94.6 proof

25. Schnapps is a liqueur.

26. Blended Canadian whisky

27. Johnnie Walker Black Label is a 12 year old blended Scotch whisky.

28. Tequila mellows and develops a golden hue when aged in wood.

29. Tonic water is another name for quinine.

30. A B-52 is made in the following sequence: Kahlúa, Baileys Irish Cream and Grand Marnier.

31. A Southern Comfort Manhattan is made with dry vermouth.

32. Straight-up refers to a cocktail prepared in a mixing set, strained into chilled glass and served without ice.

33. A Presbyterian is made with ginger ale and club soda.

34. To build a drink is to make it directly into the glass in which it is to be served.

35. A splash always means water unless otherwise instructed.

36. A Vodka Gimlet made with triple sec is a Kamikaze.

37. A Gibson is a Martini garnished with cocktail onions.

38. Sugar syrup; made with 1 part sugar and 2 parts boiling water

39. A Wine Spritzer is made with equal parts of white wine and club soda.

40. A float of Galliano turns a Screwdriver into a Harvey Wallbanger.

41. A Spritzer is made with equal parts of wine and club soda and a Cooler is made with equal parts of wine and Seven-up.

42. The Chi-Chi is made with vodka, coconut syrup and pineapple juice; the Piña Colada is made with light rum, coconut syrup and pineapple juice.

43. In case a mistake is made with the vermouth, either using too much or the wrong type, the liquor portion will not be wasted.

44. Tom Collins

45. Myers's Jamaican Rum; labeled as the "Planter's Punch Brand"

46. False — a frozen or blended Margarita is more highly diluted and therefore less potent.

47. False — the alcohol in beer and wine is naturally buffered and has a more moderate impact on BAC.

48. True

49. True

50. True

TEST TWO — INTERMEDIATE LEVEL BAR EXAM

1. Frequently confused with tequila, this smoky Mexican spirit is perhaps best known for the "little something extra" added to each bottle.

2. Made in Perth, Scotland since the 1860's, this blend has the distinction of being the first bottled Scotch whisky.

3. What ingredient in sambuca, ouzo and Pernod turns these liqueurs cloudy when mixed with water or poured over ice?

4. What whisky was introduced in 1939 to commemorate the unprecedented visit of King George and Queen Elizabeth to Canada?

5. The recipe for what renowned liqueur was purportedly brought to Scotland by Bonnie Prince Charles in 1745?

6. Drier and more potent than anisette, this semi-sweet anise liqueur is made in Greece and Cyprus.

7. This liqueur is made from black currants grown principally in the Burgundy region of France.

8. What is America's first proprietary liqueur?

9. Metaxa 5 and 7 Star brandies are produced in what nation?

10. Made from fermented sugar cane molasses in column stills, this is the world's best selling type of rum.

11. One of the most popular whiskies in the world, it has been blended in Aberdeen, Scotland, since 1801 in both a 12 and 21 year old version.

12. Known as the "Cognac of Ireland," this single malt whiskey is triple-distilled in a copper pot still and aged 9 to 11 years in used sherry oak casks.

13. This famous Scotch whisky was the first to be blended specifically for American tastes.

14. What liqueur is the modern version of Absinthe, only now made without wormwood?

15. This aromatic French liqueur was originally labeled "Triple Sec White Curaçao" until triple sec became so widely distributed.

16. Originally brewed in Czechoslovakia, it is a bottom-fermented beer, typically golden-colored, dry and crisp; it is the most widely imitated style of beer.

17. This famous flavored rum is made from coconut and Jamaican light rum.

18. This brandy is made in Normandy, France from cider apples and is aged in oak casks prior to bottling.

19. First distilled in the 1830s by Scottish immigrants, this type of whisky is made from a blend of rye, corn and barley.

20. What do Stolichnaya Citros and Absolut Citron have in common?

21. Bourbon is distilled primarily from which grain?

22. Made with top-fermenting yeasts, this type of brew is typically heavy-bodied, copper-colored (or darker), high in alcohol and most closely identified with English-style beers.

23. Most closely associated with Italy, this sweet, fortified aperitif is infused with herbs, roots, seeds, quinine and various other botanicals.

24. More than 50 distilled spirits comprise the blend of this American whiskey, which has the distinction of being the best selling whiskey in the United States.

25. Tia Maria is made from Blue Mountain Coffee beans and what distilled spirit?

26. Is Southern Comfort a liquor or liqueur?

27. What invaluable contribution to the production of bourbon is Reverend Elijah Craig credited with?

28. What is a single malt Scotch whisky?

29. What is an eau-de-vie?

30. What is the primary difference between a VS and a VSOP cognac?

31. To what product did Mr. Justerini and Mr. Brooks lend their names?

32. What is the difference between a "split" and "half-bottle" of wine?

33. This term is used to describe the thickness or consistency of a beer as perceived in the mouth.

34. Chivas Regal issued this 21 year old blended Scotch whisky in honor of Queen Elizabeth's 1953 coronation.

35. What is armagnac?

36. What is tequila distilled from?

37. This Italian aromatic liqueur is made from an infusion of bitter herbs and popularly mixed with club soda.

38. This liqueur is made from oranges, herbs and premium Canadian whisky.

39. What two major types of whiskies are marketed without an "e" in the word whisk(e)y?

40. What is the difference between a Kir and a Kir Royale?

41. How many liters is a magnum?

42. What is the purpose behind heating a snifter before serving a brandy neat?

43. What is the continental term for a liquor served on the rocks?

44. What is the difference between a liqueur and a cordial?

45. What does the term "straight up" mean?

46. What is the difference between a Madras and a Seabreeze?

47. How is a "sweet" Manhattan prepared?

48. What does the term "neat" mean?

49. What is a mist?

50. What drink requires the use of a "bar muddler" in its preparation?

51. What will club soda poured into an empty glass reveal about the glass?

52. What name is given to the combination of champagne and orange juice?

53. What is the visible indicator that citrus juice has spoiled?

54. What are the two fortified aperitif wines used most frequently behind a commercial bar?

55. If a distilled spirit is 90 proof, how much alcohol by volume does it contain?

56. What is the garnish for sambuca served neat?

57. What mixer is used to make a "Rickey?"

58. What piece of bar equipment is used to make a Pousse Café?

59. What is a cappuccino?

60. What is seltzer water?

61. What is the name of a Long Island Iced Tea made with cranberry juice instead of cola?

61. When someone orders a "Dubonnet," is the Blonde or Rouge version being requested?

63. How does the method of affixing sugar to the rim of a glass differ from that for salt?

64. How is a "short" highball prepared?

65. What is a Black and Tan?

66. There is approximately the same amount of ethyl alcohol in a normal serving of 86.8 proof whiskey, draft or bottled beer, and white table wine.(True or False)

67. When distilled spirits are consumed, blood alcohol concentration (BAC) rises faster and higher than when an equivalent amount of either beer or wine is consumed. (True or False)

68. A Manhattan served on the rocks is less alcoholically potent than a Manhattan served straight up. (True or False)

69. Approximately 80% of the alcohol consumed enters the bloodstream directly through the lining of the stomach walls. (True or False)

70. The more food present in the stomach, the more the absorption rate of alcohol is delayed. (True or False)

71. A person's disposition or mood can alter normal absorption and cause alcohol to be "dumped" into the small intestine. (True or False)

72. Over 20% of the alcohol in the blood is absorbed by fatty tissue. (True or False)

73. The brain, muscles and central nervous system achieve relatively low concentrations of alcohol. (True or False)

74. In a man of average build, BAC will predictably rise 0.02% per ounce of spirits consumed. (True or False)

75. Conventional wisdom states that anyone at a BAC of 0.1% will exhibit signs of impairment. (True or False)

76. A tall rum & cola is more alcoholically potent than a regularly prepared rum & cola. (True or False)

77. A small percentage of the blood alcohol is detoxified through evaporation in the lungs. (True or False)

78. Alcohol is detoxified primarily through the function of the liver. (True or False)

79. The human physiology detoxifies alcohol at a fixed rate of approximately one ounce every two hours. (True or False)

80. The majority of people begin exhibiting signs of impairment at a BAC of 0.1% to .15%. (True or False)

TEST TWO — INTERMEDIATE LEVEL ANSWER KEY

1. Mescal; every bottle contains a blue agave rootworm

2. Dewar's White Label

3. Oil of anise

4. Crown Royal Canadian Whisky

5. Drambuie

6. Ouzo

7. Crème de Cassis

8. Southern Comfort

9. Greece

10. Puerto Rican rum

11. Chivas Regal Scotch Whisky

12. Black Bush by The Bushmills Distilling Co.

13. Cutty Sark

14. Pernod

15. Cointreau

16. Pilsener

17. Malibu

18. Calvados

19. Canadian whisky

20. Both are Stolichnaya Citros and Absolut Citron lemon-infused vodkas.

21. Corn

22. Ale

23. Sweet Vermouth

24. Seagram's Seven Crown Whiskey

25. Jamaican rum

26. Liqueur

27. Reverend Elijah Craig was the first to age bourbon whiskey in charred casks.

28. A straight, unblended malt whisky from a single distillery

29. Eaux-de-vie are brandies, typically clear, distilled from the fermented mash of fruit or pomace, the remnants of the wine-making process and either left unaged or aged in glass vessels to retain their clarity.

30. Aging; a VS cognac is usually aged 4-5 years, while a VSOP cognac is typically aged in wood 7-10 years

31. J. & B. Rare Scotch Whisky

32. A split of wine contains 187ml, 6.35 ounces, or one-quarter of a wine bottle; a half-bottle of wine contains 375ml or 12.7 ounces.

33. Body

34. Chivas Regal Royal Salute

35. Armagnac is an aromatic, full-bodied brandy made in Gascony, France, in continuous still and aged in black oak casks.

36. Tequila is distilled from the Agave Tequilana Weber, also known as the Blue Agave.

37. Campari Aperitivo

38. Yukon Jack

39. Scotch whisky and Canadian whisky

40. A Kir is made with white wine and crème de cassis, while the Kir Royale is made with champagne and crème de cassis.

41. A magnum is equal to two wine bottles, 1.5 liters, or 50.4 fluid ounces.

42. A heated snifter causes brandy to hasten the release of its bouquet.

43. Over, as in "Scotch, over"

44. There is technically no difference between a liqueur and cordial; however, the word cordial is usually used in conjunction with the sweetest of the liqueurs.

45. Straight up refers to a cocktail prepared in a mixing set, strained into chilled glass and served without ice.

46. A Madras is made with vodka, orange juice & cranberry, while a Seabreeze is made with vodka, grapefruit & cranberry juice.

47. A sweet Manhattan is prepared with an additional quarter of an ounce of Maraschino cherry juice.

48. Neat means to serve a product undiluted and usually at room temperature; with the notable exceptions chilled vodkas, schnapps, cream liqueurs, etc.

49. A mist is a liquor served over crushed ice.

50. A bar muddler is used to "muddle" or squash the fruit garnish in an Old Fashion.

51. The carbon dioxide present within the club soda will form a stream of bubbles on the glass wherever it is oily or dirty.

52. Mimosa or Buck's Fizz

53. Natural carbonation or "spritz" will form around the inside edges of the container.

54. Sweet and dry vermouth

55. A 90 proof spirit contains 45% alcohol by volume.

56. Three roasted coffee beans, signifying health, wealth and happiness

57. A Rickey is any requested clear liquor and club soda.

58. A bar spoon is used to make a Pousse Café; each liqueur is sloped over the back of the bar spoon, slowing the force of the pour sufficient such that it layers on top of the previous liqueur.

59. A cappuccino is hot espresso coffee and a layer of steamed, frothed milk.

60. Seltzer water is synonymous with club soda or carbonated water.

61. Long Beach Iced Tea

62. Unless otherwise instructed, a call for Dubonnet means the Rouge version.

63. Water is used to affix sugar to the rim of a glass and lime juice is used to affix salt.

64. A short highball is prepared in the glass one size smaller than a regular highball glass; because of the reduced capacity of the glass, a "short" highball has a higher concentration of alcohol.

65. Black and Tan is a layered beer drink made with draught stout and ale.

66. True

67. True

68. True

69. False — approximately 10% - 15% of the alcohol absorbed enters the bloodstream through the stomach lining.

70. True

71. True

72. False — fat cells do not absorb alcohol from the bloodstream.

73. False — the brain, muscles and central nervous system achieve relatively high concentrations of blood alcohol.

74. True

75. False — some people exhibit signs of impairment as early as 0.05% BAC, while others might not exhibit symptoms of intoxication until 0.15% to .2% BAC.

76. False — tall mixed drinks are more highly diluted and therefore lower in alcohol potency.

77. True

78. True

79. False — the liver detoxifies alcohol at an approximate rate of one ounce per hour.

80. False — the majority of people exhibit signs of impairment between 0.05% and 0.1% BAC.

TEST THREE — ADVANCED LEVEL BAR EXAM

1. What small-batch, 120 proof bourbon is undiluted, unfiltered and bottled straight from the barrel?

2. The nutty-almond flavor of Disaronno Amaretto is derived from what product?

3. What is acknowledged to be the first 100% blue agave tequila imported into the U.S.?

4. Made from a blend of various Caribbean rums on the island of Tortola, this full-bodied spirit is standard issue for sailors of the British Royal Navy since 1655.

5. This famous Italian liqueur is thought to have been formulated as love potion by a coven of witches?

6. What liqueur was formulated by 16th century alchemists in Europe as a medicinal elixir?

7. What fortified wine is most closely associated with solera aging?

8. What infamous liqueur was dubbed the "Green Muse?"

9. What popular Scandinavian spirit is twice-distilled from either grain or potatoes and has the flavor of caraway?

10. What is the principal difference between a brandy and an eau-de-vie?

11. Established in 1804, this Jamaican firm produces one of the most famous brands of Demerara rum.

12. What type of charcoal is used to filter Jack Daniel's Tennessee Whiskey?

13. How do most native Canadians refer to their indigenous whisky?

14. This full-bodied brandy is made in the French province of Gascony.

15. This renowned liqueur is made from 15 year old Highland single malt Scotch whisky and heather honey.

16. Produced since 1607 by Carthusian monks, this French liqueur is made from brandy, wild mountain herbs and redistilled four times before aging.

17. In Spain, this liqueur is known as Cuarenta y Tres.

18. What is Poire William?

19. This renowned French quinine-flavored aperitif is produced in both a "Blonde" and "Rouge" version.

20. This dry, aromatic European liqueur is made from caraway, cumin and neutral spirits.

21. This Dutch juniper-infused spirit is the predecessor of London Dry Gin.

22. What do grappa and marc have in common?

23. What is the American version of prunelle?

24. This French liqueur has been made by the Carthusian monks since 1838 and is characteristically similar to Benedictine.

25. This amber, hoppy brew is considered a hybrid, being made from both top- and bottom-fermenting yeasts; it is made only in San Francisco.

26. This popular French Framboise is made from small black raspberries, herbs and honey.

27. Most closely associated with France, this aperitif wine is aged 2-3 years in oak casks exposed to the elements to accelerate maturation.

28. This highly sought-after French red wine is bottled extremely young and cannot be legally sold before the third Thursday in November.

29. Cognac is only produced in the region centered around this small town in France.

30. This Swedish vodka is infused with paprika and jalapeño pepper.

31. This award-winning Russian vodka is distilled from winter wheat and glacier water.

32. Made entirely of blue agave, this handcrafted tequila is estate grown and bottled, and aged for 2 to 3 years in oak barrels.

33. This gold medal-winning vodka is made in Belgium and distilled entirely from sugar beets.

34. The majority of Canadian whiskies contain a small amount of this product to soften and mellow the blend.

35. Made in Frankfort, Kentucky, this whiskey is considered the first single cask bourbon.

36. This famous dark, aromatic rhum is double-distilled on the island of Haiti from sugar cane juice.

37. If by law, tequila must contain a minimum of 51% agave, what constitutes the remaining 49 percent?

38. Produced in both a sweet, and a dry, bitter (Irish) version, this style of beer is typically full-bodied, dark in color and brewed using roasted, unmalted barley.

39. This orange-flavored, cognac-based liqueur was issued to commemorate the company's 150th anniversary.

40. This dry Belgian liqueur is made from Andalusian tangerines and fine aged cognac.

41. This clear aromatic liqueur is made from almonds and Dalmation Marasca cherries.

42. This renowned Cognac house is perhaps best known for their Louis XIII brandy.

43. Made in France since 1872, this French fortified aperitif is semi-dry and has the subtle flavor of oranges, herbs and quinine.

44. What is a frappé?

45. What does the mixology instruction "over and up" mean?

46. What is a "bourbon and branch?"

47. The original Manhattan recipe called for Italian vermouth, bourbon or rye whiskey, and what other ingredient?

48. The Buena Vista Cafe located at Fisherman's Wharf in San Francisco is credited with popularizing what famous hot drink?

49. What bitters is used to make a Champagne Cocktail?

50. What drink is closely associated with the running of the Kentucky Derby?

51. What is a dash?

52. What is a horse's neck?

53. What is a Black Velvet?

54. This French non-alcoholic water is perfumed with the scent of orange blossoms and is invaluable in preparing a Ramos Fizz.

55. What is the given name for a Margarita made with brandy instead of tequila?

56. What is a Shandy Gaff?

57. Which results in a lower figure, measuring a beer's alcohol content by weight or by volume?

58. What is Old Tom Gin?

59. This whiskey by Wild Turkey is a 110 proof, undiluted, unfiltered single cask bourbon.

60. This yellow-hued, aromatic vodka is only produced in Eastern Poland and flavored

with rare species of grass from which it derives its name.

61. This descriptive phrase is used to identify the small amount of whisky that is lost from a cask through evaporation.

62. What is the generic name for French anise liqueurs such as Ricard and Pernod?

63. The style of brewing associated with this city in northern Germany produces a dry, golden-blonde, bottom-fermented lager.

64. This French liqueur is made by the Lapostelle family from passion fruit and Armagnac brandy.

65. These potent German beers usually end in the suffix "-ator."

66. Brewed exclusively in monasteries in Belgium and the Netherlands, these beers are fruity, bottle-conditioned and made from top-fermenting yeasts.

67. The Stags Leap District is a renowned appellation within this famous California wine-growing county.

68. This burrowing plant louse devastated European vineyards between 1860 and 1880 and its descendants are now ravaging Californian grape vines.

69. Sheep Dip and Pig's Nose are examples of what type of spirit?

70. Where in Scotland are single malts Laphroaig and Lagavulin produced?

71. Now distilled in Pennsylvania, this 4 year old, straight rye whiskey was originally distilled in Cincinnati.

72. Glenkinchie and Rosebank are preeminent examples of single malt whiskies made in this region of Scotland.

73. What is the name used to describe very old cognacs that have been removed from their casks and placed in glass decanters for later use in blending?

74. Cragganmore and Knockando are among the finest single malt whiskies made in what region of the Scottish Highlands?

75. What rum is flavored with such items such as coconut shells, limes, roots and raisins?

76. This 86-proof Jamaican rum is aged 18 years in white oak barrels.

77. Swing is this distillery's 20 year old blended Scotch whisky.

78. This 12 year old, Highland single malt Scotch is aged in oak casks previously used to age sherry.

79. A "Fine Champagne" cognac is made from a blend of brandies from what two regions?

80. "Oude" and "Jonge" are styles of this type of gin.

81. What is Stolichnaya Okhotnichya?

82. On what island is the medium-bodied rum Cockspur distilled?

83. The pyloric valve plays a large role in determining how rapidly alcohol passes through the stomach and into the small intestine. (True or False)

84. Emotional stress, worry or anxiety may initially cause absorption rate to decrease. (True or False)

85. The more a person weighs, the less BAC rises per ounce of alcohol consumed. (True or False)

86. Body fat content has a direct impact on the rate of intoxication. (True or False)

87. A woman's BAC rises at the same rate as a man's per ounce of alcohol consumed. (True or False)

88. Since alcohol is absorbed at a constant rate, the pace that someone drinks alcohol will not affect BAC. (True or False)

89. BAC decreases at a rate of 0.015% per hour. (True or False)

90. There is nothing within reason that can increase the rate a person detoxifies and sobers up. (True or False)

91. Despite being classified as a depressant, alcohol initially acts as a stimulant on the central nervous system. (True or False)

92. Exhilaration, loss of inhibition and a sense of calm or well being are accepted indications of a high BAC. (True or False)

93. As BAC rises, alcohol acts progressively more as a depressant. (True or False)

94. After a person stops drinking, impairment will continue about 25% over the next hour. (True or False)

95. BAC usually peaks 60 minutes after a person stops drinking. (True or False)

TEST THREE — ADVANCED LEVEL ANSWER KEY

1. Booker Noe by James B. Beam Distilling Co.

2. Crushed apricot pits

3. Tequila Herradura

4. Pusser's British Navy Rum

5. Liquore Strega

6. Goldwasser

7. Sherry

8. Absinthe

9. Akvavit (aquavit)

10. Brandies are invariably aged in wood, and as such, have dark, rich color; eaux-de-vie are either left unaged or aged in glass vessels so they retain their clarity.

11. Lemon Hart Demerara Rum

12. Sugar Maple charcoal

13. Most Canadians refer to their indigenous whisky as "Rye," this despite the fact that it is distilled with a relatively small percentage of rye.

14. Armagnac

15. Drambuie

16. Green Chartreuse

17. Licor 43 — Cuarenta y Tres means "43" in Spanish

18. Poire William is a dry and aromatic European eau-de-vie distilled from a fermented mash of William, Bartlett and Anjou pears.

19. Dubonnet

20. Kümmel

21. Genever or Schiedam gin

22. Both are pomace brandies; both are made from the remnants of the winemaking process

23. Sloe Gin

24. Yellow Chartreuse

25. Steam beer is now only produced by the Anchor Brewery in San Francisco.

26. Chambord Liqueur Royale de France

27. Dry Vermouth

28. Beaujolais Nouveau

29. Jarnac, France

30. Absolut Peppar

31. Stolichnaya Gold Vodka

32. El Tesoro de Don Felipe Añejo 100% Blue Agave Tequila

33. Black Death Vodka

34. Sherry

35. Blanton Single Barrel Bourbon

36. Rhum Barbancourt

37. Caña, or distilled cane sugar

38. Stout

39. Grand Marnier Centcinquintenaire

40. Mandarine Napoleon

41. Maraschino

42. Remy Martin

43. Lillet

44. A frappé is a recipe or liqueur served over crushed ice.

45. The mixology instruction "over and up" means that the drink is to be prepared in a mixing glass over ice and then strained straight up.

46. Bourbon and branch is a highball made with bourbon and spring water.

47. Angostura bitters

48. The Buena Vista Cafe popularized the Irish Coffee

49. A Champagne Cocktail is made with champagne and a sugar cube saturated with Angostura Bitters.

50. The Mint Julep is closely associated with the running of the Kentucky Derby.

51. A dash is equal to 10 drops or 0.16 teaspoon

52. A horse's neck is a drink garnish made of the entire peel of either an orange, lemon or lime cut in a continuous spiral.

53. A Black Velvet is a drink made with stout and champagne

54. Orange flower water

55. Side Car, which is made with brandy, triple sec and sweetened lemon juice; the Margarita is made with tequila, triple sec and sweetened lemon juice

56. Shandy Gaff is made with equal parts of beer and ginger ale.

57. Measuring a beer's alcohol content by weight results in a figure 20% lower than if measured by volume.

58. Old Tom Gin is a London-style gin with added sweetening agents.

59. Wild Turkey Rare Breed

60. Zubrowka Polish Vodka

61. The Angel's Share

62. Pastis liqueurs

63. Dortmunder

64. Le Grande Passion

65. Doppelbock

66. Trappiste Abbey Ale

67. Napa Valley

68. Phylloxera

69. Scotch whisky: Pig's Nose is a blend of Highland malt and grain whiskies; Sheep Dip is an 8 year old Highland single malt.

70. Laphroaig and Lagavulin are distilled on the Isle of Islay.

71. Old Overholt Rye Whiskey

72. Glenkinchie and Rosebank are Single Lowland Malt Scotch whiskies.

73. Paradis

74. Cragganmore and Knockando are Single Speyside Malt Scotch whiskies.

75. Barbados rum

76. Appleton Estate Extra Jamaican Rum

77. Johnnie Walker Swing blended Scotch whisky

78. Glendronach Single Highland Malt Scotch Whisky

79. The Petite Champagne and Grand Champagne Cognac regions of France

80. "Oude" and "Jonge" are styles of Genever gin.

81. Stolichnaya Okhotnichya is a 90 proof, herb and honey flavored vodka.

82. Barbados rum

83. True

84. True

85. True

86. True

87. False — a woman's BAC will rise at a faster rate than a man's per ounce of alcohol consumed

88. False — rate of consumption has a significant impact on absorption rate

89. True

90. True

91. True

92. False — they are indications of a relatively moderate BAC

93. True

94. True

95. False — BAC usually peaks 15-30 minutes after a person stops drinking

SECTION 6
ANSWER KEYS

What was the
first London Dry Gin? The
majority of the world's vodkas
are distilled from what product? Where was
the Bacardi Rum distillery located before it moved to
Puerto Rico? What is the primary flavor of famed Disaronno Originale Amaretto? Where is Seagram's 7 Crown Blended Whiskey produced?
How does the pear get into the bottle of Poire William Eau-de-vie? What brand is
acknowledged as the first 100% blue agave tequila imported into the U.S.? How do
almond-flavored liqueurs derive their flavor? What liqueur was formulated by 16th
century alchemists in Europe as a medicinal elixir? What ingredient in sambuca, ouzo
and Pernod turns these liqueurs cloudy when poured over ice or mixed with water?
What whisky was introduced in 1939 to commemorate the unprecedented visit of
King George and Queen Elizabeth to Canada? What is the primary botanical in
nearly all brands of gin? With regards to the distilling of gin, what are botanicals?
What is the technical difference between lagers and ales? What is the principle
character difference between lagers and ales? What liqueur is actually a bottled gin
sling cocktail, a drink originated at a London restaurant in the late 1800s? What is the
best-selling brand of Goldwasser? The recipe for what renowned liqueur was
purportedly brought to Scotland by Bonnie Prince Charlie in 1745? What famous Scotch
whisky-based liqueur is made on the Isle of Skye? What famous American whiskey was
the first to be marketed in a square-shaped bottle? Which is aged longer, Wild Turkey
Black Label or White Label Bourbon? What famous Russian vodka is infused with lemon
essence? What product is most closely associated with solera aging? What country
does sherry originally come from? Baileys Original Irish Cream is made from chocolate,
coffee, cream and what distilled spirit? What liqueur bears the initials D.O.M. on its label?
Chambord Royale Liqueur has the rich flavor of what fruit? Other than color,
what is the principle difference between Blue
Curaçao and Triple

Section One: Product Knowledge Answers

1. Booth's has been distilling House of Lords Gin since 1740.

2. The majority of vodkas are distilled from corn; it yields more vodka per bushel than other grains or potatoes.

3. Booker Noe Bourbon distilled by James B. Beam Distilling Co. of Clermont, Kentucky.

4. Santiago, Cuba

5. Disaronno Amaretto has a pronounced nutty almond flavor with notes of orange and vanilla.

6. Mezcal (mescal); Most bottles contain a blue agave root worm.

7. It is a classic Italian liqueur made from grape spirits that are steeped in 17 herbs and fruits

8. Dewars White Label Scotch Whisky

9. The Old Bushmills Distillery in County Antrim is considered the oldest whiskey distillery having been established in 1784.

10. Lawrenceburg, Indiana

11. The bottle is attached to the branch of a pear tree such that the budding fruit actually grows inside of it.

12. Herradura Tequila was first imported into the US in the 1950s by Bing Crosby and Phil Harris.

13. Since almonds do not yield their flavor in alcohol, the oil of crushed apricot kernels are used to replicate the almond flavor.

14. Kahlúa Coffee Liqueur

15. Goldwasser

16. Pusser's British Navy Rum

17. Oil of anise

18. Glenmorangie Single Highland Malt Whisky

19. Crown Royal Canadian Whisky

20. Juniper berries

21. Botanicals are the herbs, spices, roots, berries and fruits used to flavor gin.

22. Lagers are brewed with bottom-fermenting yeasts, while ales are brewed using top-fermenting yeasts.

23. The principle character difference between the two types of beers is that ales have a fruit-laced bouquet.

24. Pimm's Cup #1

25. Liquore Strega

26. Danziger Goldwasser made in Gdansk, Poland is the best-selling brand of Goldwasser.

27. Rumple Minze Peppermint Schnapps

28. Drambuie Liqueur

29. Drambuie Liqueur

30. Ouzo

31. Jack Daniel's Tennessee Whiskey

32. Canadian Club (C.C.) Whisky

33. Wild Turkey White Label is aged for 8 years.

34. Stolichnaya Ciros Vodka

35. Stolichnaya Citros

36. Stolichnaya Gold Vodka

37. Sherry

38. Spain

39. Triple distilled Irish whiskey

40. Benedictine D.O.M. Liqueur

41. Small black raspberries

42. Triple Sec is drier than blue Curaçao

43. Creme de cassis

44. Southern Comfort

45. Absinthe

46. Akvavit (aquavit)

47. Greece

48. Cognac

49. Puerto Rican rum

50. Lager

51. Jägermeister Liqueur

52. Brandies are invariably aged in wood, and as such, have dark, rich color; eaux de vie are either left unaged, or aged in glass vessels so that they retain their clarity.

53. Vodka

54. Captain Morgan Original Spiced Rum

55. Chivas Regal Scotch Whisky

56. Chivas Regal is a blended Scotch whisky

57. The initials on the label of Seagram's V. O. Canadian Whisky stand for "Very Own."

58. Gin is flavored with botanicals, such as berries, roots, bark, seeds and plant parts.

59. Smirnoff Vodka; founded by Piotr Arsenovich Smirnoff

60. Black Bush by The Bushmills Distilling Co.

61. Cutty Sark Blended Scotch Whisky

62. Rum is distilled from fresh sugar cane juice or sugar cane molasses.

63. Myers's Original Dark Jamaican Rum

64. The majority of all brandies are distilled from a fermented mash of grapes.

65. Akvavit (Aquavit) is distilled from grain or potatoes and flavored principally with caraway.

66. Mead (metheglin)

67. Pernod Pastis

68. Sambuca

69. Grand Marnier Liqueur

70. Grand Marnier Cuvee de Cent Cinquantenaire

71. Cointreau Liqueur; created by Edouard Cointreau

72. Pilsener (Pilsner); originally brewed in Pilsen, Czechoslovakia

73. Malibu Rum

74. Nassau Royale

75. Creme de noyaux (Almond)

76. A blend of grain and single malt Scotch whiskies

77. Beefeater London Distilled Dry Gin

78. Lemon Hart Demerara Rum

79. Calvados

80. The islands in the Caribbean have climates ideal for cultivating sugar cane, from which rum is distilled.

81. The majority of all Scotch whiskies—including single malts—are blended

82. Jack Daniel's whiskey is mellowed using Sugar Maple charcoal.

83. Canadian whisky

84. Myers's Original Dark Jamaican Rum

85. Both Stolichnaya Ciros and Absolut Citron are imported, citrus-infused vodkas.

86. Corn

87. As a result of being aged in wooden casks, the insides of which have been charred, bourbons are usually darker than Scotch whiskies.

88. Ale

89. Sweet Vermouth

90. When making red wine, the skins are left in contact with the juice after the grapes have been pressed. Within the skins are pigments that give the grapes their color. These pigments, in turn, give color to the resulting wine.

91. London dry gins usually range in alcohol content between 86 and 94.6 proof.

92. Schnapps is a liqueur.

93. Boodles is a premium, 90.4 proof London Dry Gin.

94. Vodka is distilled to an extremely high alcohol content, as a result, nearly all of the congeners and particulate that give a spirit flavor and color are distilled out of it. Vodkas are also filtered to remove any remaining trace impurities.

95. Seagram's 7 Crown Whiskey

96. The Jim Beam Distillery in Clermont, Kentucky

97. Many Canadians refer to their indigenous whisky as "rye," this despite the fact that it is distilled with a relatively small percentage of rye grain.

98. Jamaican rum

99. Southern Comfort

100. Southern Comfort

101. Angostura Bitters

102. Stolichnaya Vodka

103. Reverend Elijah Craig is credited with being the first to age bourbon whiskey in charred casks.

104. A single malt Scotch is a blend of malt whiskies distilled at a single distillery in Scotland.

105. Chivas Regal is a blended Scotch whisky while Glenfiddich is a single Highland malt Scotch whisky.

106. Rum

107. An eau de vie is a typically clear brandy, distilled from the fermented mash of fruit or pomace—the remnants of the wine-making process—and left either unaged or aged in glass vessels to retain their clarity.

108. An overproof rum, such as 151-proof rum, which contains 75.5% abv

109. Armagnac

110. The main difference is the amount of aging each receives; a V.S. Cognac is usually aged 4-5 years, while a V.S.O.P. Cognac is aged in wood 7-10 years.

111. Fine Champagne cognac

112. Green Chartreuse Liqueur

113. Opal Nera

114. Liquore Galliano has a spicy, licorice flavor.

115. Licor 43, means "43" in Spanish

116. The second stage of producing gin involves redistilling grain spirits with flavoring agents called "botanicals," a reciped mixture of roots, herbs, fruits and seeds; the most dominant flavor is usually that of juniper berries.

117. Smirnoff Vodka

118. Old Overholt is an American straight rye whiskey.

119. Blended Canadian whisky

120. Tennessee

121. J. & B. Rare Blended Scotch Whisky

122. Cutty Sark Blended Scotch Whisky; the Cutty Sark was the fastest clipper ship of its day and the fastest means of transporting, among other things, Scotch whisky across the Atlantic to the United States.

123. Single malt Scotch whiskies are distilled entirely from a fermented mash of malted barley.

124. The Glenlivet is distilled in the Highlands, specifically the region known as the Speyside.

125. Demerara rum is column distilled from the molasses of sugar cane grown along the Demerara River in Guyana, South America.

126. Poire William is a dry, aromatic brandy (technically an eau de vie) distilled from a fermented mash of William, Bartlett and Anjou pears. The brandy is often marketed with a pear in the bottle.

127. A pomace brandy is usually clear, unaged or aged in glass vessels, and distilled from the grape remnants of the wine-making process. Grappa is an example of a pomace brandy.

128. A split of wine contains 187ml, 6.35 ounces, or one-quarter of a wine bottle; a half-bottle of wine contains 375ml or 12.7 ounces.

129. Dubonnet

130. Body

131. Aquavit

132. True

133. Peppermint schnapps

134. Kümmel

135. Frangelico Liqueur

136. Crème de noyaux

137. The only difference between the two versions of crème de cacao is color

138. Southern Comfort is a liqueur

139. The two famous Johnnie Walkers are comprised of different blends of whiskies. In addition, the whiskies used in Johnnie Walker Black Label are aged a minimum of 12-years, while Red Label contains some whiskies younger than that.

140. Genever or Schiedam gin

141. Queen Victoria

142. Poland

143. Made in Moscow, Stolichnaya Pertsovka is a grain vodka infused with cayenne, capsicum and cubed peppers.

144. Fresh whiskies are clear when they come out of the still.

145. Wild Turkey White Label (101 proof) Bourbon is aged in charred oak barrels for a minimum of 8 years.

146. Haig & Haig Dimple Pinch Scotch whisky

147. The Glenlivet

148. Chivas Regal Royal Salute Scotch Whisky

149. Mount Gay Eclipse Rum

150. Both are pomace brandies; they are distilled from the remnants of the wine-making process.

151. Armagnac is an aromatic, full-bodied brandy made in the French province of Gascony, France.

152. Tequila is distilled from the Agave Tequilana Weber, also known as the Blue Agave.

153. Campari Aperitivo

154. Tia Maria

155. Sambuca Romana

156. Anise

157. Pernod is a brand of pastis, a French anise-flavored liqueur.

158. What is today known as Disaronno Amaretto.

159. Curaçao

160. Southern Comfort

161. Yukon Jack

162. Irish Mist is an Irish liqueur made from herbs, clover, heather honey and Irish whiskey.

163. Crème de menthe

164. Chambord Liqueur Royale de France

165. Midori

166. Sloe Gin

167. Green Chartreuse

168. Yellow Chartreuse

169. Steam beer is now only produced by the Anchor Brewery in San Francisco.

170. Vandermint Liqueur

171. Doctor McGillicuddy's Mentholmint Schnapps

172. Licor 43 (Cuarenta y Tres)

173. Godiva Liqueur

174. Rumple Minze is a peppermint schnapps imported from the Black Forest in Bavaria.

175. Bäerenjäeger is a German, amber-colored honey liqueur

176. Bock beer

177. Fernet Branca is an aromatic, Italian medicinal bitters.

178. Dry (French) vermouth

179. Beaujolais Nouveau

180. Peychaud's Bitters

181. Tequila mellows and develops a golden hue when aged in wood.

182. The Grande Champagne district is located in the Cognac region of France.

183. Slivovitz is a potent, eastern European plum brandy

184. Eau de vie

185. Over proof rum is one containing 57.5% alcohol by volume (115 proof) or more

186. Stolichnaya Citros

187. Plymouth Gin

188. Stubbs Queensland Dry Rum

189. In the process of malting barley, the germinated grain is dried in a kiln over a peat fire, permeating the barley malt with the aroma and flavor of peat smoke, which is later imparted to the whisky.

190. Usher's Green Stripe Blended Scotch Whisky

191. Mount Vernon Rye Whiskey

192. Old Crow Bourbon

193. Absolut Peppar Vodka

194. Absolut Citron Vodka

195. Old Forester Bourbon

196. Black Death Vodka

197. Blanton Single Barrel Bourbon

198. John Jameson & Son Irish Whiskey

199. Gentleman Jack Rare Tennessee Whiskey

200. Talisker is made on the Isle of Skye

201. Black & White Scotch Whisky

202. Rhum Barbancourt

203. An American brandy distilled in pot stills from fermented cider apples. It is made by the Laird Company, the country's oldest distiller.

204. Caña, or distilled cane sugar

205. Grappa is a clear pomace brandy, usually unaged or aged in glass vessels, and distilled from the remnants of wine pressings.

206. Sherry is a blended fortified wine produced in Jerez de la Frontera, Spain, aged and blended in large oak casks by the solera system.

207. Stout

208. Framboise is a French raspberry liqueur

209. Triple sec

210. The only difference is color

211. Everclear Grain Alcohol

212. Grand Marnier Cuvee de Cent Cinquantenaire

213. Cherry Heering is named after its founder, Peter Heering.

214. Cherry Marnier

215. Mandarine Napoléon Liqueur

216. Maraschino Liqueur

217. Tuaca Liqueur

218. Malt liquor

219. Remy Martin Cognac

220. Lillet

221. The Blue Hawaiian originated at the Zanzibar Club in London.

222. "Jonge" or "Oude" are styles of Genever gin.

223. Bombay Sapphire London Dry Gin

224. Tanqueray London Dry Gin

225. Bombay Original Dry Gin

226. It is a cognac made from a blend of brandies from the Grande Champagne and Petite Champagne regions of France.

227. Absolut Kurant

228. John Jameson 1780

229. Glenfiddich Highland Single Malt Scotch Whisky

230. Sauza Hornitos 100% Agave Reposado Tequila

231. Poire William or eau de vie de poire

232. Kirsch is an eau de vie distilled in an alembic still from the fermented mash of black cherries.

233. Bombay Sapphire London Dry Gin

234. Barbados rum

235. The House of Martell

236. Aalborg

237. Poire William or Eau de Vie de Poire

238. Cognac

239. Cognac

240. Canadian Club Canadian Whisky

241. It is a spirit distilled from fresh cane juice, as opposed to molasses of cane syrup.

242. It is a blended tequila made from a minimum of 51% blue agave and 49% caña (distilled sugar cane).

243. Tequila is made exclusively in Mexico and double distilled from a minimum of 51% blue agave.

244. Brandy is a distilled spirit made from the fermented mash of grapes or fruit.

245. Rum is a spirit distilled in either column (continuous) or pot stills from sugar can juice, cane syrup or molasses.

246. Evan Williams Vintage Dated Single Barrel Bourbon

247. Chambord Liqueur Royale de France

248. Bärenjäger is a German, amber-colored honey liqueur.

249. Jägermeister is a German liqueur made from 56 herbs, roots and spices.

250. Applejack is a classic American brandy distilled from apples.

251. Bafferts

252. Van Gogh Wild Appel Vodka

253. Sauza Tres Generaciones Plata Tequila

254. Three Olives Vodka

255. Maker's Mark Bourbon

256. Herradura Selección Suprema

257. The Agave tequilana Weber, or the Weber Blue Agave

258. Tequila must be distilled a minimum of two times.

259. A reposado (rested) tequila is aged in wood for a minimum of two months, although most remain in the wood four to eight months.

260. An añejo tequila must be aged a minimum of one year in barrels 600 liters or smaller, with most aged in 180-liter, oak barrels.

261. Agavero is a tequila-based liqueur made in Mexico and flavored with Damiana.

262. Goldschläger is a cinnamon schnapps produced in Switzerland containing 24-carat gold flakes.

263. Most premium white rums are aged in oak barrels like their gold counterparts, and then they are filtered to remove their color.

264. Don Facundo Bacardi in 1862 at his small distillery in Santiago, Cuba.

265. Appleton Estate

266. Angostura 1824 Limited Reserve

267. Bacardi Carta Blanca

268. Mount Gay Eclipse Barbados Rum

269. Jose Cuervo

270. Chateau Courvoisier

271. L'Esprit de Courvoisier

272. Gosling's Black Seal Rum

273. Tequila Herradura

274. Grey Goose Vodka

275. Hpnotiq Liqueur

276. Martini & Rossi Vermouth

277. Pyrat Rums

278. Sauza Tres Generaciones Plata Tequila

279. Finlandia Vodka

Section Two: Commercial Mixology Answers

280. The more commonly used name for quinine is tonic water.

281. The Caipirissma is prepared with light rum.

282. Scotch whisky and Canadian whisky

283. When a Martini is shaken and not gently stirred, the agitation would cause the vermouth, a fortified wine, to turn the drink somewhat cloudy and opaque. Thus the descriptive phrase, "a bruised Martini," came into being.

284. A White Cosmopolitan is prepared with white grape juice instead of cranberry juice.

285. A kir is made with white wine and créme de cassis, while the kir royale is made with champagne and créme de cassis.

286. A magnum is equal in volume to two wine bottles; 1.5 liters, or 50.4 fluid ounces.

287. The combination of Angostura bitters and club soda is often used to settle an upset stomach.

288. A B-52 is made in the following sequence: Kahlúa, Baileys Irish Cream and Grand Marnier.

289. A frappé is a recipe, or liqueur, served over crushed ice.

290. A heated snifter hastens the release of the brandy's bouquet.

291. The mixology instruction "over and up" means that the drink is to be prepared in a mixing glass over ice, and then strained straight-up.

292. Bourbon and branch is a drink prepared in a highball glass made with bourbon and spring water.

293. Seasoned ice refers to the ice remaining in a person's glass after finishing a drink. Often customers will request that their next drink be built upon the "seasoned" ice.

294. A Southern Comfort Manhattan is made with dry vermouth.

295. "Over", as in "Scotch, over"

296. Angostura Bitters

297. To prove the of alcohol content, an equal amount of gunpowder and spirits were mixed together. If the mixture didn't burn, the spirit was considered too weak. On the other hand, if it burned with a steady blue flame, it was considered suitable for consumption—around 50% alcohol by volume, or 100 proof.

298. There is technically no difference between a liqueur and cordial; however, the word cordial is usually used in conjunction with the sweetest of the liqueurs.

299. Straight up refers to a cocktail prepared in a mixing set, strained into chilled glass and served without ice.

300. Bucket glass

301. A Madras is made with vodka, orange juice and cranberry, while a Seabreeze is made with vodka, grapefruit and cranberry juice.

302. Gimlet

303. A buck, chiller and highball are each made with ginger ale.

304. A Presbyterian, or "press," is made with ginger ale and club soda. It should be noted that in some areas, a press is made with lemon-lime soda and club soda.

305. A sweet Manhattan is prepared with an additional quarter of an ounce of Maraschino cherry juice.

306. Building a drink requires pouring the recipe ingredients directly into the glass in which it is to be served.

307. The term neat means to serve a product undiluted and usually at room temperature.

308. The metric equivalent of a fifth is a 750ml bottle (25.4 oz.).

309. The third sink compartment is filled with sanitizer solution

310. The term "splash" means to add a small amount of water, unless otherwise instructed.

311. The Bocci Ball is prepared with Disaronno Amaretto.

312. Dark 'n' Stormy

313. A float means to free pour approximately a 1/2 ounce of the last ingredient on top of a drink.

314. A mist is a liquor served over crushed ice.

315. 33.8 ounces

316. A vodka gimlet made with triple sec added is a Kamikaze.

317. A Martini garnished with cocktail onions is called a Gibson.

318. A bar muddler is used to "muddle" or squash the fruit garnish in an Old Fashion.

319. The carbon dioxide present within the club soda will form a stream of bubbles wherever the inside of the glass is oily or dirty.

320. Harvey Wallbanger

321. The Cuba Libre, which literally means "Free Cuba."

322. Mimosa or Buck's fizz

323. Natural carbonation or "spritz" will form around the inside edges of the juice container.

324. Dry and sweet vermouth

325. Tomato juice is added to beer to make a "Red Beer."

326. The movie version of James Bond immortalized the "Vodka Martini, shaken not stirred."

327. A 90 proof spirit contains 45% alcohol by volume.

328. Three roasted coffee beans, signifying health, wealth and happiness.

329. The Brandy Inhaler

330. Peychaud's Bitters, an anise-flavored bitters

331. Egg white

332. A pony glass is one fluid ounce.

333. The yellow, rind-side of the twist faces the glass; when twisted, the oil of essence of lemon is expressed out of the rind flavoring and adding a lemon flavor to the cocktail.

334. Adding beef bouillon to Bloody Mary mix turns it into Bloody Bull mix.

335. A Rickey is any requested clear liquor and club soda, e.g. Gin Rickey, Vodka Rickey, etc.

336. A bar spoon is used to make a Pousse Café; each liqueur in the recipe is sloped over the back of the bar spoon, slowing the speed of the pour such that product layers on top of the previous liqueur.

337. A cappuccino is hot espresso coffee and a layer of steamed, frothed milk served in a large, porcelain coffee mug.

338. Seltzer water is synonymous with club soda or carbonated water.

339. Simple syrup is the name given to sugar syrup. It is made by combining equal parts of granulated sugar and boiling water.

340. Long Beach Iced Tea

341. A Sombrero is made with Kahlúa and cream, while the Smith and Kerns is made with Kahlúa, cream and club soda.

342. A Champagne Cocktail is made with champagne and a sugar cube saturated with Angostura Bitters.

343. The standard serving portion for an aperitif wine, such as Dubonnet, is 2 ounces.

344. Downeaster

345. Moscow Mule; a highball drink made with vodka, ginger beer and a lime wedge.

346. De Kuyper Pucker Sour Apple

347. A short shaker is a stainless steel can designed to fit snugly over a collins or

chimney glass, such that the contents can be shaken directly in the glass.

348. A topless Margarita is one served without a salted rim.

349. A Red Eye is red beer with an egg yolk floating on the surface.

350. The speed rack is positioned at thigh level in front of the bartender's workstation. It is used to hold well liquor for easy and rapid access.

351. A parfait is a blended drink made with one or more liqueurs and ice cream.

352. The clock behind the bar is purposely set five or ten minutes fast to ensure that all drinks served have been removed well within legal time limits.

353. Congeners are impurities and particulate held in suspension in distilled spirits that contribute to the flavor, color and aroma of the liquor.

354. The term "dog house" refers to the back bar liquor display case.

355. A dash is equal to 10 drops or 0.16 teaspoon.

356. A flash blend is a technique of preparing a mixed drink in an electric blender. The blender is turned on for only 3-5 seconds yielding a frothy, partially frozen drink.

357. Ginger beer is a non-alcoholic, ginger-flavored carbonated beverage; most famous as the mixer in the Dark'n Stormy and Moscow Mule.

358. A horse's neck is a drink garnish made of the entire peel of either an orange, lemon or lime cut in a continuous spiral.

359. A punt or kick-up is an indentation found on the bottom of champagne bottles; also found on many cognac and wine bottles.

360. An overflow pipe is a stainless steel or hard plastic tube fitted with a rubber stopper that is inserted into the drain of a sink to maintain a constant water level.

361. If the money in the cash register drawer is less than the total of the register's sales keys minus the opening bank, the drawer is said to be "short" or "under" by that amount.

362. A Black Velvet is a drink made with stout and champagne.

363. The bar die is the technical name for the front structure of a bar.

364. The bar par is a roster of all of the opened and unopened bottles of liquor inventory stocked behind a bar at any one point in time.

365. A mist is made with a liquor poured over crushed ice and a frappé is a liqueur served over crushed ice.

366. Daiquiri

367. The Black Velveteen is made with Guinness Irish Stout and Hard Apple Cider.

368. Zombie

369. Rose's Lime Juice

370. Orgeat is a sweet almond-flavored, non-alcoholic syrup produced in France.

371. Pink gin is made by adding several dashes of Angostura Bitters to chilled gin. The drink was originally made with Plymouth Gin.

372. A liquor gun is a hand-held electronic device that, with the assistance of a built-in micro-processor, dispenses a predetermined measure of liquor.

373. Flaked ice is finely crushed or shaved ice.

374. A float of Liquore Galliano will turn a tall Screwdriver into a Harvey Wallbanger.

375. Grenadine syrup is flavored with pomegranates.

376. Orange flower water

377. Unless otherwise instructed, a call for Dubonnet means the Rouge version.

378. A Spritzer is made with equal parts of wine and club soda and a Cooler is made with equal parts of wine and 7-up (lemon-lime soda).

379. The Chi-Chi is made with vodka, coconut syrup and pineapple juice, while the Piña Colada is made with light rum, coconut syrup and pineapple juice.

380. The phrase "86 someone" originated during prohibition. If a customer in a speakeasy became intoxicated, the management would instruct the bartender to serve the person 86 proof spirits instead of the 100 proof.

381. The combination of gin and dry vermouth is called a Gibson when it is garnished with cocktail onions.

382. The Manhattan debuted at a gala function held at the famed Manhattan Club.

383. Tiramisu

384. Bacardi Cocktail

385. The Screwdriver

386. The Mickey Finn

387. King Alphonse

388. Collins mixer is essentially sweetened lemon juice and club soda.

389. Shandy Gaff is made with equal parts of beer and ginger ale.

390. Water is used to affix sugar to the rim of a glass and lime juice is used to affix salt.

391. A short highball is prepared in the glass one size smaller than a regular highball glass; because of the reduced capacity of the glass, a short highball has a higher concentration of alcohol.

392. Breakage refers to the liquor and liqueur bottles emptied during the course of a day's bartending shift(s).

393. In states where it is legal to bring a bottle of wine into a restaurant, a corkage fee is a surcharge added to the patron's bill for the house opening and serving the wine.

394. It is a restaurant term for a table set with two place settings

395. French 75 is a cocktail made with gin, sweet 'n' sour and champagne.

396. French 75 is a cocktail made with gin, sweet 'n' sour and champagne, while the French 125 is made with cognac instead of gin.

397. In the event too much vermouth is used, or the wrong type of vermouth is used, the liquor portion will not be wasted.

398. An "orange flag," a half-moon orange slice and a speared cherry, is the standard garnish on a whiskey sour.

399. Tom Collins

400. Myers's Original Dark Jamaican Rum

401. Heating a coffee glass prior to service prevents breakage due to thermal shock and also helps keep the drink hotter longer.

402. Gomme syrup is the French name for simple syrup, or sugar water.

403. A Black and Tan is a layered beer drink made with Guinness Irish Stout and Bass Ale.

404. A tall highball is prepared in the glass one size larger than a regular highball glass; because of the increased capacity of the glass, a tall highball has a lower concentration of alcohol.

405. A Caipirinha is a rocks drink made with cachaca, simple syrup and lime juice.

406. Very Superior (or Special) Old Pale

407. Gin and Sweet Vermouth

408. A Mudslide is made with vodka, Kahlúa and Baileys Irish Cream.

409. The Mojito is a drink that originated in Cuba and is made with crushed mint leaves, sugar, lime juice and a measure of light rum.

410. The side car, which is made with brandy, triple sec and sweetened lemon juice; the margarita is made with tequila, triple sec and sweetened lemon juice.

Section Three: What's Your Alcohol IQ Answers

411. False — a frozen or blended Margarita is more highly diluted and therefore less potent

412. True

413. False — The alcohol in beer and wine is naturally buffered and has a more moderate impact on BAC.

414. True

415. True

416. True

417. True

418. False — there is a direct relationship between rate of absorption and the onset of intoxication

419. False — Approximately 10% - 15% of the alcohol absorbed enters the bloodstream through the stomach lining.

420. True

421. True

422. True

423. True

424. False — BAC rises slower and peaks at a lower point when alcohol is consumed with a meal.

425. False — fatty foods tend to decrease the absorption rate

426. False — Foods that are high in carbohydrates are easily digested and tend to increase the alcohol absorption rate.

427. True

428. True

429. False — carbonation tends to increase the absorption rate

430. True

431. True

432. False — fat cells do not absorb alcohol from the bloodstream

433. False — The brain, muscles and central nervous system achieve relatively high concentrations of blood alcohol.

434. True

435. True

436. True

437. False — A woman's BAC will rise at a faster rate than a man's per ounce of alcohol consumed.

438. False — rate of consumption has a significant impact on absorption rate

439. False — the higher the proof, the faster the onset of intoxication

440. False — Some people exhibit signs of impairment as early as 0.05% BAC, while others might not exhibit symptoms of intoxication until 0.15% to .2% BAC.

441. False — Tall mixed drinks are more highly diluted and therefore lower in alcohol potency.

442. False — Beer and wine have a more moderate impact on the physiology than do distilled spirits.

443. True

444. True

445. True

446. False — The liver detoxifies alcohol at an approximate rate of one ounce per hour.

447. True

448. False — Detoxification occurs at a fixed rate and is unaffected by rate of consumption.

449. False — detoxification is unaffected by the type of distilled spirits consumed

450. True

451. True

452. True

453. False — they are indications of a relatively moderate BAC

454. True

455. False — The majority of people exhibit signs of impairment between 0.05% and 0.1% BAC.

456. True

457. False — BAC usually peaks 15-30 minutes after a person stops drinking.

458. True

459. True

460. True

461. True

462. True

463. True

464. True

465. False

466. True

467. False

468. False

469. True

470. True

471. False

472. True

473. False

474. True

475. False — The bartender should not prepare the second drink until that person's age or sobriety are established.

476. False — Management conventionally only reserves the prerogative to overrule the decision to proceed with service.

477. False — refusal of service should occur well before that point

478. False — the bartender should proceed and deny further service

Section Four: Questions for Seasoned Pros Answers

479. Measuring a beer's alcohol content by weight results in a figure 20% lower than if measured by volume.

480. Alt or Dusseldorf Alt

481. Old Nick Martinique Rhum

482. Old Tom Gin is a London-style gin with added sweetening agents.

483. Wild Turkey Rare Breed

484. Lambic

485. Zubrowka Polish Vodka

486. To qualify as bottled bourbon held in bond, it must be a straight bourbon whiskey, aged a minimum of 6 years and 100 proof.

487. Porter

488. Bierre de Garde

489. George Dickel & Co.

490. The Angel's Share

491. Kriek

492. Old Medford New England Rum

493. Linie Aquavit

494. Also known as "Brussels Lace," it refers to the beer foam that sticks to the inside of a glass as the head recedes; a sign of a good beer and clean glass.

495. Aguardiente is distilled from sugar cane or molasses, occasionally made from grapes, and typically bottled without aging or rectification.

496. Pastis liqueurs

497. Pronounced "klawck", the initials of the Danish Kümmel C.L.O.C. stands for "Cuminum Liquidium Optimum Castelli."

498. Saison

499. Chocolat-Suisse Liqueur

500. Chartreuse V.E.P. Liqueur

501. Prunelle

502. Dortmunder

503. Munchener

504. Fraise is a French eau de vie made from wild strawberries.

505. Praline Liqueur

506. Irish Mist

507. Hoegaards Wit

508. Hazelnut

509. Barley Wine

510. Himbeergeist is a Eastern European raspberry liqueur

511. Le Grande Passion

512. Mozart Nougat Cream Liqueur

513. Eiskümmel

514. Oktoberfest

515. Moët Petite Liqueur

516. Cordial Medoc

517. Doppelbock

518. Creme de Yvette (a.k.a. Creme de Violette)

519. Canton Delicate Ginger Liqueur

520. Izarra

521. Russian Imperial Stout

522. Goldwasser derives its predominant flavor from coriander

523. Earl Grey Liqueur

524. Trappiste Abbey Ale

525. Berliner Weisse

526. Falernum

527. Advokaat

528. Parfait Amour

529. Swedish Punsch

530. Mild Ale

531. Bitter Ale

532. Napa Valley

533. Phylloxera

534. Scotch whisky: Pig's Nose is a blend of Highland malt and grain whiskies; Sheep Dip is an 8 year old Highland single malt

535. Laphroaig and Lagavulin are distilled on the Isle of Islay.

536. Tanqueray London Dry Gin

537. Tarkhuna Georgian Vodka

538. Old Overholt Rye Whiskey

539. Glenkinchie and Rosebank are Lowlands single malt Scotch whiskies.

540. Paradis

541. Cragganmore and Knockando are Speyside single malt Scotch whiskies.

542. Barbados rum

543. Johnnie Walker Swing Blended Scotch whisky.

544. Wray and Nephew Jamaican Rum

545. Glendronach Single Highland Malt Scotch Whisky

546. "Oude" and "Jonge" are styles of Genever gin

547. Stolichnaya Okhotnichya is a 90 proof, herb and honey flavored vodka.

548. Tanqueray Sterling Vodka

549. Asbach Uralt Brandy

550. Applejack

551. A bottle of XXO (Extra, Extra Old) cognac

552. Cachaça

553. Marc is a French brandy distilled from pomace—the remnants of the wine-making process.

554. Shochu

555. Aguardiente

556. Cachaça is a dry aguardiente (sugar cane distillate) made primarily in Brazil.

557. V.O.V. Liqueur

558. Ketel One Vodka

559. Bonn and Cologne, Germany

560. Ojen

561. Yellow Chartreuse

562. Ricard

563. Brontë Yorkshire

564. John Jameson and Son

565. Havana Club is a range of continuous distilled rums made in Havana, Cuba.

566. Glenmorangie Côte de Nuits Wood Finish

567. Crater Lake Vodka by Bendistillery

568. Conch Republic Rum

569. Distillers' Masterpiece Bourbon

570. Germain-Robin Anno Domini 2001 Brandy

571. Laird's 12-year-old Rare Apple Brandy

572. Teton Glacier Potato Vodka

573. McKendric Western Style Whiskey

574. Ultimat Vodka

575. Boru Vodka

576. Doorly's X.O. Barbados Rum

577. Sea Wynde Pot Still Rum

578. Old Raj Dry Gin

579. Hendrick's Gin

580. El Tesoro de Don Felipe Paradiso

581. Kelt XO Tour du Monde Cognac

582. Danziger Goldwasser

583. Knappogue Castle Irish Whiskey Vintage 1951

584. Malt Liquor

585. Canadian Club Sherry Cask Whisky

586. Blavod Black Vodka

587. Citadelle Gin by Cognac Ferrand

588. McLain & Kyne Jefferson's Reserve

589. McCarthy's Oregon Single Malt Whiskey

590. A. H. Hirsch 16-Year and 20-Year Bourbon

591. Highland Park Orkney Single Malt

592. A. Hardy Perfection Grande Champagne Cognac

593. Bushmills Black Bush

594. Chivas Century of Malts Blended Scotch Whisky

595. Beefeater Gin

596. Old Overholt Rye Whiskey

597. Johnnie Walker Gold Label

598. Hennessy

599. Blanton's Single Barrel Bourbon

600. Midleton Very Rare Irish Whiskey

601. Glenmorangie 10-year-old Single Malt

602. Stolichnaya Gold

603. Talisker 10-year-old Single Malt

604. Rhum is the french word for rum: on the islands that were former French colonies rhum is distilled from unfermented sugar cane juice and referred to as Rhum agricole.

605. Wild Turkey Kentucky Spirit

606. Rhum Vieux are aged a minimum of three years in barrels no less than 650 liters in capacity.

607. Rhum Vieux are aged a minimum of 3 years and Rhum Trés Vieux are barrel aged at least 10 years.

608. Goldschläger

609. Crème de Noyaux

610. Blue Curaçao

611. Agavero Liqueur

612. Triple Sec

Answers to "What's All the Brouhaha about Beer" *Test page 7*

1. Dust, dirt or salt will make the head on a flat beer reappear.

2. None, beer is brewed, not distilled

3. Prolonged exposure to direct sunlight or fluorescent light causes a photochemical reaction that will adversely affect the beer's taste and create an offensive odor.

4. The internal pressure within a sealed bottle doesn't not allow the carbonation within the beer to form bubbles.

5. Should the pressure within the CO2 lines exceed 14 p.s.i. the beer will be over-carbonated and come out wild and foamy.

6. If the pressure within the CO2 lines falls below 12 p.s.i. the beer will lose its carbonation and come out flat.

7. If the temperature of the draft beer drops below 36°F the beer will come out flat.

8. If the temperature of the draft beer raises much above 38°F the beer will come out cloudy, and wild and foamy.

9. Lagers are a style of beer brewed using bottom-fermenting yeast.

10. Ales are a style of beer brewed using top-fermenting yeasts.

11. The beer foam that sticks to the inside of a glass as the head recedes; a sign of a well-crafted beer and a clean glass.

12. The Japanese brewery Kirin; Kirin Dry

13. Barley malt, hops, yeast, water

14. Ice beer is chilled until ice crystals form, which are removed, thereby reducing the beer's water content and elevating its percentage of alcohol.

15. Hops are a climbing vine that when brewed produce tannins that help clarify and preserve beer.

16. Yeasts are used in the brewing process to initiate fermentation.

17. Barley is a grain that, when steeped in water, germinates and provides the source of fermentable sugars for the brewing process.

18. Krausening is a brewing process of adding young beer to brewing lager to cause a second fermentation.

19. A well-crafted beer produces a tightly knit, dense, uneven head comprised of small, uniform bubbles.

20. Lambic beer is a spontaneously fermented wheat beer made in and around the city of Brussels, Belgium.

Answers to "What's Your Tequila IQ" *Test page 11*

1. The Agave tequilana Weber, or Weber blue agave.

2. After 8-12 years the agaves contains the highest amount of residual sugar. It is that sugar that is eventually fermented into alcohol.

3. With the leaves trimmed away, the agave's core resembles a pineapple, or *piña*.

4. After the piñas are split into quarters, they are baked in a hornos (oven) to convert the plant's natural starches into fermentable sugars.

5. The *aguamiel* is transferred to a large fermentation tank. Water and yeast are added to the tank to start fermentation.

6. During fermentation, the juice boils as the sugars are slowly converted into alcohol and carbon dioxide.

7. The fermented juice is transferred to either a pot still or continuous still.

8. Tequila must be distilled a minimum of two times.

9. A reposado (rested) tequila is aged in wood for a minimum of two months but less than a year, although most remain in the wood four to eight months.

10. An añejo tequila must be aged a minimum of one year in barrels 600 liters or smaller, with most aged in 180-liter, oak barrels.

11. El Tesoro Paradiso is a blend of El Tesoro silver and añejo 100% agave tequilas extended aged in De Fussigny Cognac casks.

12. Del Dueño Jerezito Añejo is made from select casks of Del Dueño 100% Agave tequila that are transferred into sherry pipes and allowed to it to further mature for an extended period.

13. A *mixto* tequila is one that contains less than 100% agave. They are produced from a blend of agave and distilled cane sugar.

14. XXX Siglo Treinta is a blended—mixto—tequila made with 51% agave.

15. A *hornos* is a large stone oven used to bake the agaves converting the plant's natural starches into fermentable sugars.

Answers to "How's Your Linkages with the Past" *Test page 31*

1. Bellini

2. Bloody Mary

3. Keoki Coffee

4. French 75

5. Martini

6. Mai Tai

7. Old Fashioned

8. Irish Coffee

9. Blue Hawaiian

10. Ernest Hemingway

11. Tom Collins

12. Zombie

13. Manhattan

14. Micky Finn

15. Kir

16. Piña Colada

17. Professor Jerry Thomas

18. Prairie Oyster

19. Daiquiri

20. Mint Julep

Answers to "What You Might Not Know About Beer" *Test page 46*

1. Pilsener; the original being Pilsner Urquell

2. Balance

3. Steam; sole domain of Anchor Brewing Company

4. Degrees Balling is commonly used in Europe to measure the amount of fermentable material present in a beer prior to fermentation; such a figure directly relates to the finished beer's alcoholic content.

5. Lager

6. Porter; including Labatts, Anchor, Ballantines, Boulder and Timothy Taylor

7. Ale

8. Krausening is the brewing practice of adding younger beer to a lager in the process of brewing to cause a secondary fermentation.

9. Nose

10. Lambic; including Lindemans, Liefmans, Girardin and Timmermans

11. Japan

12. Bock

13. Stout; including Guinness, Beamish and Mackeson

14. Malt Liquor

15. Oktoberfest

16. Mild Ale

17. Bitter Ale

18. Trappiste Abbey Ale; including Chimay, Orval, Westmalle and St. Sixtus

19. Berliner Weisse; including Berliner Kindl Weisse and Schultheiss

20. Dortmunder; typified by Dortmunder Actien (DAB) & Dortmunder Union (DUB)

21. Munchener; including Augustinerbraü, Korschungs and Hofbraühaus

22. Kriek; including Liefmans, Timmermans and Vanderlinden

23. Bierre de Garde; including Jenlain, Lutèce and Rimaux

24. Saison; including Dupont and Saison Silly

25. Hoegaards Wit; typified by DeKluis Brewery

Notes

Notes

Notes

Notes

Notes

Notes